I0116779

Novel Published By: A.R.Hilton

ISBN# 9780615436500

Printed in the U.S.A.

Copyright 2014

Published 2014

Edited By: Carla M. Dean, U Can Mark My Word

Graphics By: Baja Ukweli

"There is no difference between the two; the dealer cannot exist for long without becoming the killer."

Elias

"But at what cost?"

Prophecy of a Hustler II

(A War of Souls)

CHAPTER 1

Inside the snow-covered parking lot of a small shopping complex in Pelham, which was bordered by Mount Vernon and the Bronx, Kamari parked his Jeep Cherokee. Four months had passed since the shooting at the Red Parrot, an incident that stemmed from Kamari misjudging his control of a situation because he was too personally involved with both parties. However, in the wake of it all, things went on pretty much the same, as was the case when Kenny was murdered. It is said that on the streets the loss of a package shook things up more than the loss of a life, unless that life belongs to the man who supplies everybody.

For Kamari, the only setback for him in terms of business was the arrest of Big Mike from School Street on an attempted murder charge. He had beaten some dude damn near to death for smacking some female he was dealing with. In his absence, though, he put Kamari on to his man whom he was working with. As for Kamari's personal life, he was still seeing Erica, along with a new female he had met from

4

Yonkers named Shelly. Then there was Tasheeva, who sometimes visited him.

Climbing out of the jeep with him was Marco, who he picked up from his girlfriend's apartment in New Rochelle. They hadn't seen much of Oscar lately because of some job he got working with a friend of his father's out in Queens. With Christmas only two days away, the shopping complex was crowded. Kamari wanted to get a gift for Erica, so they made their way around to the jewelry store. At the entrance, they waited for the owner, who Kamari knew, to buzz them in. The buzzer sounded, and they went inside.

"Give me a minute, and I'll be right with you," said Frank, the owner, as he tended to a customer.

"Take your time," replied Kamari, as he and Marco went over to the display counter that ran the length of the store.

Frank had five attractive females that worked for him and his partner. Four of them were white, and the fifth Asian. They were between the ages of nineteen and twenty-two, and they all seemed fascinated by Kamari, who was unlike anyone they had ever met in the predominantly white suburb of Pelham in which they lived. To them, Kamari, with his money, the way he dressed, and his air of confidence, represented something new and exciting, something unknown and forbidden. For him, the attention was

5

welcomed. However, he was so entrenched in his own world that he gave little, if any, thought to venture outside of it on any level, not even for pleasure.

"What can we help you with today?" asked the smiling Asian female from behind the glass counter.

"I'm looking for something for a female, a bracelet or something," he answered, gazing through the display glass.

"How about these?" she said, pulling out an assortment of gold bangles and bracelets from under the counter.

As he was looking at them, Frank came over.

"Now, what is it you're looking for?" said Frank, coming to a stop beside the Asian female.

"He wants a bracelet for a woman," she answered.

"Is it for Christmas?" inquired Frank, looking at Kamari.

"Yeah."

"A girlfriend?"

"Something like that," he replied, smiling.

6

"You have to excuse him. He's been hurt before," said Marco, nodding toward Kamari.

"He doesn't look like the type who's easily hurt," replied the Asian female, while smiling at him.

"All that's just a shell of who he really is," responded Marco.

"Is that so?" she said, staring inquisitively at Kamari.

"Don't pay him no mind," he said, giving Marco an elbow. "Yo, Frank, what you got for me in the back?"

"I have something back there you should like," he said, before disappearing to the back.

When he returned, Kamari and Marco were speaking to the Asian female and the blonde worker who had joined them in his absence.

"Here you go," he said, stepping between the two females and handing Kamari a bracelet.

"What is it, white gold?" he asked, holding it up for a closer inspection.

"Yes," answered Frank. "It's a charm bracelet. You can add charms as gifts for any occasion. You can order them or have them specifically made to fit the occasion," he continued, as

Kamari fiddled with the three charms that were already on the bracelet.

There was a teddy bear, a heart, and a butterfly all made of white gold and encrusted in diamonds on a rather simple chain.

"What do you think?" he asked, turning to Marco.

"It's unique," he said, inspecting it.

"And it becomes even more unique as you add charms," said Frank.

"Wrap it up nicely for me. I'll take it," he said, reaching into his pocket, unconcerned with the price.

"Whoever she is she's going to love it," remarked the blonde.

"She better," Kamari said, arching his brows as he followed Frank to the cash register.

CHAPTER 2

"Hey, yo, Tubah, where you got your stash at?" asked Moose, talking to a heavyset brown skin kid standing before him on Seventh Avenue by Ebony Gardens.

"Why?" he asked, while glancing around and finding his answer. "Yo, Fue, what you doing, man? Get the fuck outta here," he shouted at Fue, a crackhead who hung around the projects and Ebony Gardens looking for dealers' stashes.

"I ain't doing nothing," he said, scanning the ground and kicking at a crumbled brown paper bag.

"Yeah, you ain't doing nothing a'ight," yelled Tubah, taking a kick at him, but missing and almost falling to the ground, which was slippery from the snow. "Goddamn you, Fue!" he shouted, catching himself as Fue took off toward the projects, while Moose stood by laughing. "Shit ain't funny, Moose. You could have grabbed him for me. I'ma beat that nigga's ass if he come back around here again."

"What I'ma grab him for? You wanted him off the block, right?"

"Yeah, that was before I almost busted my ass," he said, laughing himself. "Now I wanna whoop his ass then run him off the block," he added, as Kamari came down the block and parked on the corner in front of them.

Shutting the engine, he got out wearing a pair of black corduroys, a tan Champion sweatshirt with a tan Woolrich snorkeler, and some wheat- colored Gore-Tex boots.

"What's up, Moose?" he said, walking over to them. "Tubah, what happened? I thought you was going to get with me this morning?" he continued, coming to a stop beside Tubah, the newest member of his team who worked out of 7th Avenue and the projects.

"Fucking with those niggas little Russ and them, acting like fools out here last night, busting off guns for nothing. Made the block all hot and shit," Tubah replied.

"Y'all don't have to worry about that nigga doing no shit like that again," said Moose.

"Why?" asked Tubah.

"His uncle Fuss had work out here last night. So when he finds out a nigga still sitting on his shit and why, you can bet he gonna get in that little nigga's ass."

"He better, because if a nigga outside the family do it, it won't be pretty."

"So what's it looking like right now?" asked Kamari.

"It's so-so right now, but I should be ready to see you before the day is out. Shit, it's Christmas. You know that heads was laying on Santa's ass," Tubah said, smiling.

"Yeah, one of them tried to sell me a brand-new VCR earlier, but a nigga already got like four of them," confirmed Moose, while Kamari stood vaguely listening as he watched a black Alfo Ramiro with tinted windows pull up behind his jeep.

"Merry Christmas, niggas," said Mink, leaning back in the seat, smiling as the passenger window lowered.

"Man, you can't be rolling up on niggas like that," said Moose, as him and Tubah approached along with Kamari.

"Yeah, a'ight, I'll remember that as long as you remember not to let nobody else roll up on you like this," he said with a smirk, while leaning out the window.

"What's up, Shonda? You keeping my nigga outta trouble?" said Kamari to Shonda, who was behind the wheel.

"Kamari, this nigga don't listen to nobody but the devil. Ouch," she hollered, as Mink playfully pinched her on the leg. "See what I'm talking about, Kamari?" she said, punching Mink in the arm.

11

Watching the two of them, Kamari smiled as he thought back to the night Mink had been shot. Shonda earned a place by his side for being there for him that night.

"Fucks up with you back there, all quiet and shit?" said Kamari to Dave, who sat slouched down in the backseat.

"Nothing, just chillin'," he replied flatly.

He had taken Stagg's death the hardest. He was not as outgoing as he used to be. He took everything serious, appearing always to be in deep thought. No more dumb questions he was known for asking. It was like Stagg's death had bought to him a new outlook on life that he was struggling to grasp.

"So, Shonda, what this nigga get you for Christmas?" asked Kamari, leaving Dave to ponder whatever the death of his friend placed on him.

"Kamari, you don't even want to know," she replied, shaking her head sadly.

"What! You better tell him, and act like you appreciate my gift," Mink said, turning to her and giving her a nudge.

"Yeah, tell me. I wanna know," Kamari said, curious to know if Mink was capable of spending money on a female.

"He let me drive his new car," she said, frowning.

"And she looks good doing it, too, don't she?" Mink said, smiling at her as everybody laughed except Dave.

"He ain't shit, Kamari," she remarked, as Tubah and Moose went to tend to some heads, one of whom was trying to sell a bell cut three-quarter mink coat.

"Yo, Kamari, you wanna buy a fur for one of your girls?" yelled Tubah, sending the head with the coat over to him.

Taking the coat from him, Kamari looked it over.

"This shit is nice. It'll look good on you, Shonda," he said, while smiling at Mink who shot him daggers in return.

"Yeah, right," she replied with a laugh.

"Let me see that shit," Mink said, holding out his hand as Kamari passed it to him. "How much you want for it?" he asked the head who stood next to Kamari.

"Well, that's a ten thousand dollar coat, and it's brand-new," said the head, who was short, slim, and dressed in sweats and an old sheepskin.

"I didn't ask you all of that. I asked you how much you want for it," he said, staring at him through the open window.

13

"I want at least half of that."

"What! Five thousand dollars!"

"That's right."

"Are you fucking crazy?" Mink shouted. "I'll give you $250.00 and some crack."

"Man, let me get my coat. I don't smoke crack. I do dope, heroin," he said, reaching out for the coat, which Mink held draped over the car door.

"A'ight, I'll give you five hundred."

"Look, man, you in this nice ass ride and you wanna bicker with me about the price of my shit? Let me get my shit so I can get up out of here," he said, again reaching for the coat.

"Who the fuck do you think you talking to? I'll get out this car and murder your dope fiend ass," he shouted, looking at him with a murderous look that made him freeze up, as Dave rolled down the back window ready to make a move.

"Mink, would you please give that man back his coat," Shonda said pleadingly.

Mink stared at him for a few seconds. Then, with a smile, he handed him the coat.

14

"Thank you, brother," he said, walking away.

"Why every time you get ready to fuck a nigga up they start talking that 'brother' shit," Mink said, as Dave rolled his window back up. "I hate that shit."

"Okay, Mink, that's it enough drama for me. Can we go now? I got my mother waiting for me to help her cook," exclaimed Shonda.

"Yeah, a'ight, let's go. Kamari, I'ma catch up with you later."

"A'ight," Kamari said, backing up from the car.

"Bye, Kamari," Shonda said, pulling off and passing the head with the mink coat as he walked down 7th Avenue toward 4th Street Park.

Pulling up in front of her building, Shonda got out, as did Mink and Dave. Walking around to the driver side, Mink gave her a kiss, while Dave got in the front seat. As soon as she was in the building, Mink threw his car in reverse, coming to a screeching stop beside the head with the coat. By the time he decided to run, it was too late. Dave was out the car, grabbing him in a chokehold and dragging him into the backseat of the car. After Dave closed the door, Mink pulled off.

Kamari, who watched the whole thing, was not surprised. He knew Mink well enough to see it coming, and it came easier since he got shot and the death of Staggs.

CHAPTER 3

"You want something to drink?" Kamari asked Shelly, who sat at the kitchen table of his mother's house talking to Dahlia.

"Sure, I'll take some," she answered, referring to the two liter of soda he removed from the refrigerator.

Pouring a glass, he handed it to her.

"Happy birthday," said his mother, appearing in the doorway.

"Thank you, Ma," he replied, introducing her to Shelly, which was a first since he never formerly introduced none of his female friends to his mother, not even Natasha. Maybe it was because none of them ever asked before Shelly.

"Shelly, would you like something to eat?" asked his mother.

"No, thank you. I ate shortly before coming here, but thank you for offering," she answered with a warm smile.

"Well, if y'all would excuse me, the little one needs me," she said, hearing the baby crying in the next room.

"The little one!" exclaimed Dahlia, frowning up her face. "Mommy, stop showing off," she added.

"Dahlia, I ain't paying you no mind," replied her mother, with a frown of her own and a wave of her hand as she went to tend to the baby.

"Dahlia, you are crazy, girl," said Shelly, smiling at her.

"I always get my mother like that when we have company. She don't pay me no mind, just like she said. So where y'all going when y'all leave here?"

"Why," replied Kamari.

"Because I wanna go."

"Not this time."

"Why? Where you going?"

"None of your business."

"Shelly, where y'all going?" his persistent 14-year-old sister asked, turning to Shelly.

"Dahlia, I don't even know, but I don't see any reason why you can't come along," she said, smiling over at Kamari.

"I said not this time, next time."

CHAPTER 4

After saying their goodbyes to his mother, Kamari and Shelly headed to his apartment, which he had to himself. His aunt and her daughter had gone up north to spend the weekend in a trailer with her husband.

On the way over to his place, they picked up some ice cream, and Shelly had him take her to a bakery in Yonkers where she bought him a strawberry-filled birthday cake. However, they weren't in the apartment more than five minutes when Kamari got a call from Blass and had to run out to meet him, leaving Shelly alone in the apartment while he did so.

Entering the apartment upon his return, he smiled as he glanced into the living room at Shelly and closed the door behind him.

"What?" she said, smiling up at him from the sofa, where she laid with an Ebony Magazine open before her.

"I see you made yourself at home," he said, while going over to her, lifting her legs, and placing them across his lap as he sat down on the sofa with her.

While he was gone, she had indeed made herself at home by stripping down to nothing but the beige button-up blouse with panties and bra on underneath. Shelly, who was

20

nineteen and leggy, had the grace of a swan and mannerism of an aristocrat. Her skin was the hue of rich chocolate, and her facial features distinct with almond-shaped brown eyes, a delicate nose, hair that draped her face like that of the Egyptian Queen Cleopatra, and full lips that he found so sensuous on females. Her look was almost feline in an exotic way, with her petite frame adding to that image.

"Well, I feel at home," she purred, picking at the buttons on her blouse.

"Listen, I'm not complaining. You can take it all off," he said, rubbing her bare legs.

"Why don't you prepare the bed, because it's time to give the birthday boy his cake and ice cream," she said, closing the magazine, getting up, and going into the kitchen.

Kamari got up and made room for the pullout couch, which he opened up, and then he began to disrobe.

"Here we go," said Shelly, returning with a plate of ice cream and a piece of cake with a candle in it, as Kamari was taking off the sweatpants he was wearing.

"Come on and make a wish, then blow out the candle," she said, sitting on the side of the bed as he climbed on top in his boxers and moved over to her.

Sitting up beside her as she held the plate before him, he closed his eyes and blew out the candle.

"Now hold it," she said, handing him the plate of cake and ice cream as she stood and began removing her blouse.

"Where is the fork?" he asked, noticing she had not brought one.

"We don't need one," she said, now standing before him in red lace panties and a bra.

After tossing her blouse to the floor, she took the plate from him with one hand, while pushing him back on the bed with the other. Climbing on the bed with the plate in hand, she straddled him at the waist. Peering down at him enticingly, she took a cream- covered strawberry in her hand, placed it between her lips as she bent over, and kissed him, pushing the strawberry into his mouth with her tongue. Sitting back up, she sensuously ran her tongue over her top lip and bit her lower lip as she gazed down into his eyes. Excited, Kamari reached out for her breast.

"No," she said, guiding his hands down to his side with her free hand. "No touching until I say so," she scolded, taking some cake and ice cream and spreading it all over his chest.

She then placed the plate down beside them on the bed and began licking the cake and ice cream from his chest.

"Mmm... Mmm...," she moaned with every lick, looking up at him as he raised his head to get a better view of her in action.

Once she'd removed all of the cake and ice cream from his chest with her tongue, she began to remove his boxers, brushing against the tip of his aroused penis with her chin and licking it on her way down as she pulled his boxers completely off. Reaching over to the plate, she took a scoop of ice cream and smeared it up and down his swollen member, causing him to jump at its coldness, which was quickly replaced by the warmth of her tongue as she licked away the ice cream before taking him into her mouth.

"Ahhh... Shit," he breathed through clenched teeth, enjoying the warm pleasure as she took him over the top in her mouth.

Once he climaxed, Kamari took was left of the cake and ice cream, and smeared it over her small perky breasts and the folds of her pussy lips as she lay beside him. Starting with her breast, which had long hard nipples, he took them slowly into his mouth and bit them lightly while also teasing them with his tongue.

"Shhh... Ahhh...Yesss," she moaned in pleasure, as he licked, nibbled, and bit her breasts before burying his head between her thighs.

Taking hold of his head, she wrapped her legs around his neck and arched her back, giving him her entire pussy to work with without any interference from the mattress. After she climaxed several times, he moved up and positioned himself to enter her.

"Happy birthday," she breathed, gazing up into his eyes and kissing him as he slid inside the silky walls of her tight pussy. "Ohhh... Yesss...I'm yours. Ahhh...this pussy and me. It's yours...your gift from me... take it," she cried out as she gyrated her hips in response to his thrusts taking him completely inside of her.

They marveled in the pleasures of each other's bodies well into the night before falling asleep exhausted.

CHAPTER 5

Rolling over onto his stomach, Kamari answered the ringing phone and listened to the operator ask would he except a collect call from Mike.

"Yeah," he said, and waited for the operator to put the call through.

"Yo, Kamari, can you hear me?" shouted Big Mike.

"Yeah, nigga, I hear you. What's up?" he answered, rolling over onto his back and glancing over at Shelly, who was lying next to him with her nakedness partially exposed as she slept with the covers hanging off her sculpted body.

"Yo, these phones be fucked up and shit."

"It ain't nothing. What's up?"

"When was the last time you seen that nigga Vic?"

"The day before yesterday. Why? What's up?"

"I don't know. That's what I'm trying to find out. He was supposed to take my sister some money last week, but he didn't do it."

"He told me he was taking care of you."

"Taking care of me! I ain't heard from the nigga in almost two weeks," Mike said, his tone edged with anger.

"Did you try calling him?"

"Yo, K, I've been trying to reach the nigga ever since my lawyer told me he ain't bring the money to him."

"You think he's ducking you?" Kamari asked, as Shelly woke up and smiled over at him.

"Yo, K, I don't know what's going on. Is he taking care of business with you?"

"Yeah, so far, but fuck that. If he ain't doing right by you, he ain't doing right by me," he said, while watching Shelly get up and walk naked to the bathroom.

"Yo, you a good nigga, K."

"Yo, don't worry. How much was he supposed to take the lawyer?"

"Twenty- five hundred."

"Yo, I'm on it, kid. I'ma go see him today. Call me tomorrow morning around this time. You need anything?"

"Nah, I'm straight on the books. My girl be taking care of that."

"The one you caught this case over?" he asked, as Shelly returned from the bathroom, climbed back in bed next to him, and began caressing his dick in her hand.

"Yeah, she doing the right thing."

"Give me her number, and call her to let her know that I'ma be getting at her with something for you. Hold on, let me get a pen," he said, grabbing one from the end table along with a piece of paper. "A'ight, what's the num--," he said, trailing off as Shelly took his dick in her mouth.

"Yo, what's up, K? You a'ight?"

"Yeah, yeah, it ain't nothing. Give me the number," he answered, trying to sound normal.

"Yeah, I hear you," Big Mike said, laughing as he gave him his girl's name and number.

"A'ight, I got you. Don't worry. Just call tomorrow," he said, hanging up as Shelly picked up her pace.

Falling back on the bed, taking a deep breath, and closing his eyes, he thought to himself how he wouldn't mind waking up to this kind of treatment every morning.

CHAPTER 6

Vic drove up in his red Volkswagen GT Gulf in front of a hot dog spot in Getty Square. Getting out, he looked around for Kamari, but he had not arrived yet. It was a little past noon, and Getty Square, which the locals called The Square, was crowded with people on their lunch breaks and noonday shoppers. The Square was Yonkers' equivalent of The Avenue in Mount Vernon, a shopping district near the hood.

Walking over to the outside service window, which was open despite the cold weather, Vic ordered two franks and a hot chocolate. He hadn't been expecting to hear from Kamari for another day or two. So, when he got a call from him that morning asking him to meet him at The Square, it threw him. When he inquired what it was about, Kamari responded by simply saying that was the purpose of the meeting. The tone he used left Vic feeling a bit uneasy. He knew then that it had to be about Big Mike and the fact that he hadn't been holding up on his end of their deal. Paying for his order, he walked back to his car while glancing down the street for Kamari, who still there was no sign of. Placing the hot chocolate on the hood of his car, he leaned up against it and began eating his franks.

Fuck Big Mike. For one, the stupid motherfucker got himself locked up over a bitch, and second, the nigga didn't even want to plug me into Kamari, he thought. *I had to beg the nigga to promise me the world and shit. Yeah, fuck that nigga ! If he was really my man, it shouldn't have went like that. He was supposed to do it on the strength so a nigga can eat. But, no, because he's fucked up, he wants me to be fucked up with him. Well, fuck that,* he thought to himself.

As he finished off the rest of his franks and picked up the hot chocolate, Kamari pulled up across the street from him. Vic had been so caught up in his thoughts that he didn't see him pulling up. Hearing the Jeep door slam, he turned around to see Kamari crossing the street toward him.

"What's good?" he said as Kamari reached him.

"You tell me," replied Kamari, stepping on the sidewalk beside him.

"What you mean by that?" he asked, half-smiling.

"I'm saying, what's up with the things you was supposed to take care of for Big Mike?" Kamari replied, looking him in the eye.

"Oh, that's what this is about? I thought it was something major," he said, his half smile turning into a full smile.

"When niggas don't keep their word, it is major."

"Yo, look, K, it's about timing. Some things came up with the family that needed to be taken care of, but that's taken care of now. I'ma set Big Mike straight this time around."

"Well, you need to let him know these things, because he's been trying to catch up with you."

"I know. My people be telling me he called, but I've been missing him. I'ma lay for him, though, and let him know what's up."

"A'ight, I'ma tell you like this. The business we do ain't about me and you. It's about me and Big Mike, then you. So, if you take him out of the picture, there's nothing joining us. And if we have nothing joining us, we have no business," he said, making his point clear.

"Yo, we good, man. I'm telling you, K, we good," he added, no longer smiling.

"Yeah, a'ight. So how you lookin'?"

"A day or two, and I'ma be ready to see you again," he answered, with a confident shrug of his shoulders.

"A'ight, make sure you get that money to his lawyer before you get at me, because that's gonna be what I wanna hear the next time I see you," he said, patting him on the side of the arm and heading across the street to his Jeep.

30

Watching him get in his Jeep and pull off, Vic took a sip of his hot chocolate, which was no longer hot.

"Fuck you and Big Mike. It's my time now," he said, throwing the cup of hot chocolate to the ground as he got in his car and peeled off.

CHAPTER 7

Blowing the horn again, Mink watched the front door of the house, but still no one came out. Getting impatient, he gave the horn three rapid blows, holding it for several seconds on the third one. As he let up off the horn, Dave emerged from the house in a pair of gray cargo shorts, a sweatshirt, and a pair of Stan Smith Adidas with no socks. Coming down the porch steps, he walked over to the passenger side, opened the door, and slid into the seat, leaving the door open.

"What's up? Close the door, nigga. It's cold out here, and what was you doing that took you so long?" Mink asked, staring across at Dave as he shut the door.

"I got this bitch upstairs," he answered, nodding toward the house.

"Which one? I know her?"

"The bitch Candy that lives down the block."

"The one you said been sweating you since you moved on this block," he said, twisting up his face.

"Yeah," he replied, avoiding eye contact with him.

"Yeah, so you was up in it or what?" Mink asked, arching his brows.

"Nah, not yet."

"A'ight, what you need? A minute, two minutes? Go ahead and handle your business. I can wait," he said with a grin, trying to get a laugh out of Dave, something Dave had not done since Stagg's death. An effort that again fell short, as Dave said nothing in response. "Yo, I'm just fucking with you, my nigga. Just call me when you're ready to hang out."

"A'ight," he answered, while opening the door and getting out just as his sister Sandy came out the house.

"Mink, hold up!" she yelled, running up to the car and jumping in the front seat before Dave could close the door. "Excuse me," she said, glancing up at him as she closed the door.

Paying her no mind, Dave turned and went back into the house.

"Drop me off at my girlfriend's house," Sandy said, turning to Mink, who was staring at her like she was crazy.

"What the fuck do I look like, a fucking cab?" he cursed, as she sat staring at him with her hair pulled back in a ponytail, exposing her girlish face.

33

"You don't have to be a cab to give me a lift."

"That's how you made it sound, jumping in my shit telling me to take you somewhere."

"Okay, Mink, I'm sorry. Could you please drop me off at my girlfriend's?" she asked, while smiling at him.

"That's better. Now get the fuck out and take it from the top," he said, motioning with his thumb and turning away from her.

"Mink, come on now, shoot," she cried, pouting.

"A'ight, I'ma let it slide this time," he said, starting the engine and pulling out.

"Thank you," she said, while sitting back in the seat and twisting up her mouth when he wasn't looking.

"Where does she live?"

"In New Rochelle."

"Where in New Rochelle?"

"Take Lincoln Avenue, and once we get in New Rochelle, I'll direct you," she answered, glancing at him as he drove, while trying to figure out a way of bringing up what was on her mind. "Mink, remember when you were in the hospital?" she said, pausing.

"How the fuck can I forget? I almost died," he said, looking over at her like she was stupid, which didn't go unnoticed by her.

"You didn't give me a chance to finish what I was saying. I'm talking about the time I came to visit you with my brother and that girl," she said, knowing her name but not wanting to use it. "The one that was there with you?"

"Yeah, what about her?" he asked, not looking at her.

"I hear that's your girl now."

"You believe everything you hear?"

"No, that's why I'm asking you."

"She's the girl whose voice I heard calling me when I was dying," he answered, still not looking at her as he drove, which was something she was grateful for because he would have seen the hurt in her eyes.

Turning away from him, she asked, "Can I see you later?"

The question was her way of saying she understood and would accept being second.

"Sure, beep me and I'll come get you."

CHAPTER 8

Kamari and Marco sat in the living room of Oscar's house watching the movie Scarface, which Oscar threw in the VCR every time they got together at his house. Then there were the times they would get together at Kamari's or Marco's, and he would offer to bring Scarface for their viewing pleasure, which they always refused, saying that was for his crib only. With Oscare being Cuban and Colombian, Kamari understood his connection with the movie. It represented both sides of his ethnic background, even though it was a negative one. The movies that represented this type of connection for Kamari were Black Caesar and Hell up in Harlem, which is part two of Black Caesar. It was about a young boy in Harlem working for the Italian mob, who ran the drugs, prostitution, and gambling, as well as most of the top social clubs in Harlem at the time. He ends up going to prison for his dealing with the mob, and when he comes home, he runs them out of Harlem and takes over its criminal underworld, becoming Black Caesar. For Kamari, Black Caesar was to him what Scarface was to Oscar.

"Yo, bee, bee, here comes Marco's part," yelled Oscar, while pointing at the screen, which showed Al Pacino, who played Scarface, sitting in the hot tub of his mansion watching television. "Yo, bee, here it comes. Check it out right now. Look a da pelican. Fly, pelican, fly," Oscar said, mimicking Al Pacino as they all laughed.

"Fuck you, Oscar, you big head motherfucker," said Marco in response to the pelican scene, which was a joke shared between the three of them, making a comparison between the size of Marco's nose and the pelican's beak.

"Fly, pelican, fly," he repeated, laughing.

"You knew this part was coming," Kamari said, laughing. "Why you ain't go to the bathroom or something? You always sit through it, knowing what this motherfucker gonna do. Look, he's rewinding it," he shouted, laughing and pointing to Oscar who had the remote and was rewinding the video on the low as he sat next to Marco on the sofa grinning.

"Oh, it's like that, boulder head? Give me that," shouted Marco, trying to wrestle the remote from his hand.

Marco, who was the same age as Kamari, was six feet tall with olive colored skin. He had black curly hair that he wore faded around the sides and curly on top. Thick black eyebrows that gave him a look of seriousness when he wasn't smiling shaded his eyes, which were brown. At 18, he had a mustache and hair on his chin, and though his nose was somewhat big, it wasn't obvious. It fell in line with the rest of his features, which amounted to looks that females found appealing.

"Yo, y'all gonna break the remote," Kamari said in tears from laughing so hard, as he watched them wrestle over the remote on the sofa beside him.

Oscar, who was only 5'5", had a head that was too big for his body, and because he smoked so much weed, he always looked like he was about to fall asleep. He had a small mouth, with full lips adorned by a mustache, which was black like the long hair on his head. Females usually described him as cute in an innocent way, a description influenced by his looks as well as the shyness he displayed in their presence.

"Oh, you think this is funny," said Marco, finally freeing the remote from Oscar, but talking to Kamari, who responded by laughing even harder. "Shit is funny, huh, inner tube lips?" he said, referring to the size of Kamari's lips, and making Oscar, who was high as usual, laugh.

"At least, I have lips. You got bologna slices for lips, motherfucker," Kamari shouted back, making Oscar laugh even harder.

By now, Oscar was on the floor crying, he was laughing so hard.

"Yo, bee, y'all killing me," he said, holding his stomach and looking up at Marco.

"What the fuck you laughing at, you helium head bastard," Marco said, as him and Kamari burst out laughing.

"Yo, bee, what are you saying?" Oscar asked, turning serious.

"Yo, *head*quarters, go *'head* with that bullshit. Get it? Go *'head*," Kamari said, bringing him and Marco to tears.

"Nah, fuck that. What's up with that bastard shit?" he asked, looking up at Marco from the floor where he sat.

"You sure know how to fuck up a good time," Marco said, getting up. "I'm going to get something to drink."

"Me, too. You need to stop smoking that shit," Kamari said, passing him as he followed Marco to the kitchen.

"Yo, bee, I'm saying though-" he started to say in his defense, but left it alone and went into the kitchen after them.

In the kitchen, they gave him the silent treatment as they guzzled cans of soda, making him feel uncomfortable in his own home.

"Damn, bee, I'm sorry y'all, but…"

"It's a'ight, you plus-size head motherfucker," Kamari cut him off, and they all started laughing.

"Yo, a'ight, bee. Y'all got me," he declared, laughing.

"Yeah, it's a'ight," replied Kamari. "So what's up with this dude you been working for?"

"Yo, bee, he's major; Cali cartel," Oscar said, opening his eyes wide for a brief second.

"Yeah, is that right? So what do he be having you doing?" asked Marco.

"I drive him around to Long Island from Queens. Wherever he needs to go."

"What's up in Long Island?" Kamari inquired.

"Yo, bee, shit is crazy. They have warehouses out there where they keep keys of coke. I drive him out there with another dude, who comes with us to drive back a car that's packed with coke waiting for us. It's our job to follow him and make sure he gets to the stash house in Queens with the coke.

"You'd better be careful," said Kamari.

"Yeah," added Marco.

"I don't touch nothing, bee. Estoy en compania del jefe," replied Oscar in Spanish, while smiling.

"What the fuck does that mean?" asked Kamari.

"He's with the boss," answered Marco.

CHAPTER 9

Coming to a stop at a light on the corner of 124th Street and 2nd Avenue in Harlem, Kamari said more to himself than to Joel, who sat beside him in the passenger seat, "Oh shit!"

"What? What happened?" asked Joel, looking in the direction of Wagner projects between 124th and 123rd, the direction Kamari was staring.

"See that female over there?" he said, pointing to a strikingly beautiful, dark-skinned female in jeans, a red and blue Polo goose jacket, and a pair of Gucci boots, who was standing in front of the projects talking to a little boy. "Chew's cousin used to fuck with her."

"I don't know Chew's cousin, but that bitch is bad as a motherfucker," answered Joel, as the female walked up to a gold 190 Mercedes Benz that was double-parked and got in the passenger seat.

"Yeah, I know," Kamari said in a low voice, taken by the sight of her, just as he had been the night he'd seen her sitting on the sofa at Rome's apartment.

She had been off limits then, but that wasn't the case now. Rome had been found murdered in Virginia a month later.

They said it was in retaliation for his part in the robbery and murder of a local dealer out there.

When the light turned green, Kamari pulled alongside the Benz, getting out in a pair of faded blue jeans and a black Champion sweatshirt that he wore with a white t-shirt hanging out from beneath it. On his feet, he wore a pair of black Timberland Chucks, along with a three-quarter length black leather that swung open as he walked between the front end of the Benz and his jeep, staring at her through the windshield. Watching him approach, she rolled down the window as he came up to the passenger side door.

"Excuse me, what if I told you I knew you from someplace, but I can't remember where? Would you forgive me?" he asked, resting a hand on the hood of the car.

"What if I told you I ain't give a fuck? Would you forgive me?" she answered, flashing him a false smile.

"What if I told you I don't wanna talk, and that I just wanna fuck? Would you forgive me?" he shot back with a genuine smile.

"What if I told you you're shit out of luck 'cause I've just been royally fucked," she said, her smile now one of amusement.

"I'd say it don't count if it wasn't by me," he answered, as a light- skinned female came from out a store across the street and climbed into the driver's seat.

"Who's this, girl?" asked the light-skinned female, glancing past her at Kamari.

"Some nigga with a smart-ass mouth," she answered, staring up at him and smiling as he stared down at her, smiling back.

"Nah, I just know what I want, and if verbal wrestling is what it takes to get it, then so be it," he interjected, grinning.

"Is that right?" she replied, dipping her chin and smirking as she squinted up at him. "I guess it's true then what they say about men loving the chase."

"I guess so."

"Well, you better get in that jeep of yours, because the chase is about to begin. Let's go, girl," she said, tapping her friend who started the car.

"What, are you serious?" he said, leaning with both his hands on the door.

"You better hurry up, or else you're going to lose what you want," she replied, smiling as they pulled out into the 2nd

Avenue traffic, leaving him standing there watching as she motioned out the window for him to follow.

"She's outta her fuckin' mind if she thinks I'ma chase her ass," he said to himself as he watched them disappear in the direction of downtown.

"What's up? Why you standing there looking crazy?" Joel yelled, hanging out the passenger window.

Kamari didn't answer. Turning around, he saw the little boy she'd been talking to playing with a few other kids out in front of the projects.

"Yo, little man," he called out, pointing to him as he moved toward the projects. "Yeah, you," he said when the boy, who looked to be around twelve years of age, questioned if it was him Kamari was calling by pointing to himself. "You know Ameina?" Kamari asked when the boy came over.

"Yeah," answered the boy, staring up at him.

"Do she live in this building?" Kamari continued, pointing up at the Wagner projects.

"Yeah," he replied, nodding.

"Can you show me where?"

Staring up at him, the boy didn't answer.

"A'ight, I'll give you a dollar," he said, reaching into his pocket and peeling off a buck from the knot of bills.

Still, the boy said nothing.

"Okay, ten dollars," he said, trying to hand him the money, but he wouldn't take it. Getting the feeling that the little boy had done this before, Kamari said, "Look, this is my final offer."

He then held a twenty-dollar bill out to him.

"Okay," the boy quickly said, taking the money and stuffing it in his pocket, an act which made Kamari laugh as he followed him into the building.

They rode the elevator to the fourth floor, where her apartment was located. Kamari made him earn his money by knocking on the door to confirm that she lived there. When an older woman, who appeared to be her mother, answered the door, the boy asked for her at the amusement of the woman who told him she wasn't home. Kamari, who stood out of sight a few doors down watching, was satisfied. With a smile on his face, he turned and headed for the elevator.

CHAPTER 10

It was close to ten o'clock in the evening, when Kamari turned into the parking lot of Gorton High School in Yonkers to meet with Vic who beeped him an hour ago, informing him that he was ready to see him. Kamari had been out with Erica at the time, and wanted to put it off until the next day when he could have Lexio take him. He did not like driving dirty, even though there were times when he did due to the fast pace of the game, which sometimes demanded immediate action for the fastest turnover. It was all about the flip. Therefore, when Vic said it was moving around his way, Kamari was not going to be the reason for a slow flip.

Entering the parking lot, he could see Vic sitting on the hood of his car waiting. As he pulled in beside him, Kamari reached under the seat for the brown paper bag containing five grand worth of nickels before getting out.

"What's up? I hope you took care of that thing with Big Mike," Kamari said, coming to a stop in front of him.

"You know what? Fuck Big Mike!" Vic said, jumping down from the hood of his car as two dudes with guns drawn came out from somewhere around Kamari's jeep.

Kamari didn't have to look to know they were there. He knew what was coming from Vic's first three words.

"You see, Big Mike took himself out of the picture, and I don't do charity," he continued, while walking to within inches of Kamari's face, as Kamari stood staring at him, saying nothing. "It could've been about me and you...well, for a minute anyway, because I have bigger plans that don't include you. You see, it's about me and me only," he said, snatching the bag of crack from him and smiling as he looked inside. "Well, it was nice doing business with you, and thank you for everything you gave me," he added, holding the bag up to Kamari's face as he nodded at one of the two dudes for him to begin searching Kamari.

Assessing the dude searching him, Kamari figured him to be the hungry type, who was down for whatever as long as he got fed. Lindsay had told him in their time together that these types of individuals were the best recruits for a successful rise to the top, which told him that Vic was serious about what he was doing. Removing Kamari's money and keys from his pockets, he tossed them to Vic.

"Now, I'm going to tell you like this," he began, imitating Kamari's conversation to him days earlier. "Stay out of my town," he said, pausing and staring at him. "What you waiting for? Get the fuck out of here.

"Give me my keys," Kamari said, not attempting to conceal his anger as he stared at him.

"What nigga! Get the fuck out of here before I take your life," he yelled, as one of the dudes hit Kamari over the back of the head with the butt of his gun, knocking him to his knees.

On the ground, Kamari touched the back of his head and drew back blood, as Vic handed the keys to his jeep to one of the dudes who got inside and started the engine. Climbing into his own car along with the second dude, he backed out of the parking space and drove out of the lot, followed by the dude in Kamari's jeep.

Rising unsteadily to his feet, Kamari stood still and waited for his head to stop spinning before exiting the parking lot. Holding his head, he could feel a steady flow of blood running down the back of his neck and into the jacket he wore, soaking his shirt. Being familiar with the area, he walked a couple of blocks over to Lake Avenue, where Shelly lived with her parents. He was relieved to hear her voice over the intercom system asking, "Who is it?" He gave his name and she buzzed him up. When he reached her apartment, she was waiting in the open doorway, wearing a pair of powder blue terrycloth shorts, a t-shirt, and bedroom slippers.

"What a surprise. I was just..." she trailed off, taking one look at him and falling silent.

"Shelly, where's your parents? I need to use the phone," he said, walking up to the door, while still holding his head, his hand covered in blood.

"Oh my God, Kamari, what happened to you?" she asked, taking his face between her hands and turning his head so she could look at the back of it.

"I got robbed. Now where's your moms and pops? I need to get to your room."

"It's all right. They're in their room. Come on," she said, bringing him inside and leading him to her bedroom, where she closed the door behind them.

"Have a seat. You want to call the police?"

"Nah, no police," he quickly answered, still standing as she looked at him questioningly, but he offered nothing further.

"All right then, just have a seat," she said, pointing to the bed.

"Look, just give me the phone. I don't want to get blood on your bed," he replied, looking around for the phone.

"Don't worry about that. Just sit down," she commanded, guiding him down on the bed.

"Pass me the phone," he said, pointing to the phone sitting on her dresser.

"Alright, already," she said, bringing him the phone. "Now let me take a look at your head and get you cleaned up. I'll be right back," she said, leaving the room and closing the door behind her.

Once she was out the door, he beeped Mink and hung up to wait for his call.

Returning, Shelly proceeded over to the bed with a basin of warm water and a washcloth. "Take off your jacket," she said, helping him out of it.

Doing as she said, he balled up the shirt and held it in his hand, as he sat thinking about the things he could have done to avoid what had just happened and what he was going to do to Vic once he caught up with him. Shelly, who kneeled on her knees behind him on the bed to clean the wound on the back of his head, was doing some thinking of her own that ended with questions she knew better than to ask.

"You might need stitches," she stated, as the phone rang and he immediately answered it.

"Yeah," he said into the receiver. "Yo, I need you to come and get me. I'm in Yonkers. Some niggas robbed me and took my jeep...yeah...the 400 block of Lake Avenue... yeah, a'ight I'ma be out front waiting," he ended, hanging up.

"Let me get one of my father's shirts for you," she said, directing him to hold the washcloth to the back of his head.

She returned moments later with the shirt, which he put on while she changed into a pair of yellow sweats with a matching hoodie and some Nike running sneakers so she could go with him downstairs to wait. Standing out in front of her building, conversation was at a minimal due to the circumstances that brought him to her home. So, she understood it was best to leave him alone with his thoughts. They were out in front of her building for nearly thirty minutes before Mink arrived in his black Alfo Ramiro Milano, along with Dave. Kamari thanked Shelly with a kiss and a promise to call her the next day, before climbing into the back of the car and shutting the door as they pulled off.

CHAPTER 11

The visiting room of the Valhalla County Jail in Valhalla, New York was anything but big enough to compensate for the hundreds of inmates held behind its walls and those coming to visit them. On this day, Kamari sat amongst the visitors with Big Mike's girl, Darlene. Though he had not paid her much attention back when they first met, he could tell that becoming Big Mike's girl had been a move up the ghetto social ladder for her, as she sat stylishly dressed in designer clothes and a blue fox coat waiting on her man.

Big Mike entered the visiting room smiling for the benefit of his girl, whose face lit up as she stood and greeted him with a kiss. Turning to Kamari, who also stood, his smile was replaced with an apologetic look that Kamari acknowledged with a nod as they took their seats, which were separated by a counter that divided inmates from visitors.

"Baby, your sister wanted to come up, but I told her that your friend was bringing me up and that it would be better if she came next time," explained Darlene.

"You did right. What about the car notes? Do you have enough to stay up on them?" he asked, holding her hand.

"Well, I haven't made a payment yet because we're paid up several months in advance."

"Yeah, I didn't know that."

"I did it with the money you won gambling the night I came through to get your keys 'cause I lost mine," she reminded him, smiling.

"I forgot all about that."

Big Mike and Darlene discussed a few more things before he asked her to excuse him so that he could be alone to talk business with Kamari. They said their goodbyes, and she went outside to wait.

"First, I want you to know that I took care of the lawyer. He said the kid being in critical condition is making it hard to get you out on bail," Kamari said, moving over to the chair Darlene vacated so he could speak low while still being heard.

"Yo, that's cool, K, but I'm sorry. I didn't see the cross in the nigga," Big Mike said, sounding disappointed in himself.

"It's a'ight. I ain't see it neither."

"Nah, but I knew the nigga for years. I'm supposed to know."

"Look, you ain't the first nigga to be betrayed by a motherfucker close to him. This shit's been going on since the beginning of time. So, you won't be the last. The question now is where the fuck can I find this nigga?"

"I've been calling around since I spoke to you, and from what I'm hearing, he don't stay with his peoples no more. As far as him hustling on School Street, he must have somebody out moving his shit, because nobody's seen him around there. And the two kids you described that was with him must not have been from Y.O. At least that's what I'm hearing from the streets."

"So, basically, what you're telling me is that nobody knows where the fuck he is, no girlfriend or nothing, huh?" Kamari said heatedly.

"The nigga's a pretty boy; he runs through bitches. But don't worry. I got people looking out for him. He'll pop up. What about your jeep? Did it turn up?"

"Yeah, what is left of it."

"Yo, K, I feel fucked up about putting you onto this nigga."

"Make it right by putting me on to him again," Kamari replied, standing to leave.

"Definitely, I'm just mad that I won't be there to be a part of it when it goes down," he answered, nodding as he stood and embraced him.

"Be the part that gets it started," Kamari said, before turning and leaving.

CHAPTER 12

Ever since the incident with Vic, Kamari's mood remained somewhat solemn. He felt violated, and the longer he waited for Big Mike to come through with the information that would lead them to Vic, the more upset he got. With him, it's always been about image and respect. Respect was the foundation on which one rose in the street, allowing him to create his image, which in turn would earn him even greater respect and all the fruits that came with it. What Vic had done was a total disrespect, and though only a few people knew, it didn't matter. He knew, and for him, that was enough to tarnish his image. That's why when the word finally came down from Big Mike where they could find Vic, it was more than just business; it was personal.

At 1:30 a.m., after spending the day doing what was necessary to confirm the information, Kamari, along with Dave, sat out of sight in the back of a black stolen Mazda caravan. They were parked two houses down from a house on Warburton in Yonkers, where Vic was staying on the first floor. The front driver's side door opened, and Mink climbed in, tossing his burglary tools onto the passenger's side floor.

"I didn't even need these. The living room window was cracked. I opened it enough for us to slide through. Let's go."

Dressed in jeans, dark-colored hoodies, and sneakers, they exited the van. Walking two houses up, they turned into the fenced house and went around to the side. At the open window, they put on black ski masks and gloves before drawing their guns. Mink entered through the window first, and then Kamari followed by Dave.

Inside the apartment, there was little light, but it was easy to see that he had just moved in. There was only a couch and television in the center of the living room. To the left was the kitchen, and straight ahead to the right of the front door was a hall, which was narrow and dark, being that there weren't any windows. At the end of it was a closet with sliding doors, and on the left side just before the closet was a bathroom with its door ajar and the light out. The only other door was in the middle of the hall to the right, and as they approached it, they could hear voices coming from within. Coming to a stop outside the door, which a low glow illuminated from beneath, they listened.

"You like it rough, don't you, bitch?" they could hear Vic saying, followed by a female's moans. "Whose bitch are you?" he went on, as Mink slowly turned the doorknob and swung it open.

Vic had a female's leg up over his shoulders, pounding away, as they ran into the room and surrounded the bed. Looking up and seeing three masked dudes in his room with guns, Vic rolled off the female, who screamed when Mink struck Vic in the head with his snub-nose .357. The naked sight of Darlene surprised Kamari. Walking over, Dave backhanded her across the face, sending her halfway off the bed.

Mink quickly cuffed a dazed Vic's hands behind his back, while Dave did likewise to Darlene, who was crying hysterically.

"Here, this should shut you up," Mink said, picking her panties up from the floor and stuffing them in her mouth. "Stay in here with the bitch," he said to Dave, as he and Kamari escorted a naked Vic stumbling down the hall to the bathroom.

Turning on the light, Kamari struck Vic in the head, which was already bleeding from the blow Mink gave him, and pushed him into the tub.

"I'm only going to ask you this one time, because I don't have time to waste. So, with the right answer, you live. Give the wrong one, and you die. Now where's the money?" Mink said, leaning over the tub with both hands resting on the rim.

Vic didn't have to know who the man was behind the mask, or his reputation to know he meant every word he said; it was in his eyes.

"It's under the kitchen sink inside a plastic bag in a bucket," he answered, as Mink stood upright and exited the bathroom.

Vic knew that the other dude now standing over him was Kamari, but he was not going to say anything that might seal his fate. He knew now that he had made a mistake by not killing him. Mink returned with the plastic bag of money along with a pillow he picked up from the bedroom, and nodded to Kamari, who removed his mask.

"Hay, now you want to take off the mask," Vic said, trying to stay calm as he stared up at him, but knowing what was coming, he silently prayed for a way out.

"The mask was just to make you think it was a simple robbery, but it's a planned homicide," Kamari said, taking the pillow from Mink.

"Wait! Wait, man! I let you live, and this is what I get?" he pleaded.

"You didn't let me live. What you did was tell me you didn't know who you were fucking with," Kamari answered, while

61

placing the pillow over his head as he thrashed back and forth.

Putting the barrel of his .38 against the pillow, he fired three bullets into Vic's head, and the tub began to fill with blood.

"What's up with the girl?" asked Mink, as Kamari turned toward him.

"She's Big Mike's girl."

"What! Dirty bitch! So what do you wanna do? The nigga might've told her about robbing you, which she could tell the police," he said to Kamari, who seemed unsure.

"Don't let her know it's coming," he answered, picking up the bag of money and walking out of the bathroom.

When they got to the door of the bedroom, Kamari grabbed Mink by the arm and handed him the .38, not wanting him to use the .357 that would've took her head off.

Waiting outside the door, he told himself that it was her fault. Moments later, two muffled shots sounded inside the room, followed by Mink and Dave coming out into the hall, pulling off their masks. Putting on their hoods, they walked out the front door of the house in silence, each with his own thoughts about what they had just done.

CHAPTER 13

On the fourth floor of the Wagner projects, Kamari stood in a gray Paragon sweat suit and his black chucks outside of Ameina's apartment and knocked.

"What's up? Is the chase over?" he asked, smiling at Ameina, who opened the door in socks and a pair of form-fitting blue jeans with a brown and beige knitted sweater.

"Now how did you--" she started to say, but was cut off by him.

"Yo, let's not go through this again. My name is Kamari, and I'm just tryna get up with you, so what's up?"

She stood looking him up and down, with her hair hanging free and her breathtaking beauty sucking up all his air in the urban setting.

"Yeah, I guess the chase is over. I'm Ameina," she said, smiling as she invited him inside, where she introduced him to her mother, who was in the kitchen cooking.

Together, they sat on a sofa in the living room. "So where are you from since you don't want to tell me how you found out where I live?"

"Mount Vernon," he answered, ignoring the second part of her question.

"Mount Vernon? Ain't that where that rapper Big Joop is from?"

"Yeah," he answered, half laughing.

"Why are you laughing?" she asked, smiling quizzically over at him.

"Nah, that's always the first thing that comes out of people's mouth whenever I tell to them I'm from Mount Vernon. I tell you what. Why don't you get your coat, and I'll show you where Mount Vernon is at."

"Okay, give me a minute," she said, getting up and leaving him in the living room. Moments later, she called out, "I'm ready," from the living room doorway.

To her attire, she added a pair of black riding boots, a black leather jacket, and a cute little black hat pulled down over her ears, with her hair hanging out from under it.

"I'll see you later, Ma," she said, as her and Kamari walked out the door.

Exiting the elevator, Kamari admired the shapeliness of her behind as she walked ahead of him. Outside, she looked around for the jeep he had been driving when she met him.

"Where is your jeep?" she asked.

"Oh, you remember that," he replied, walking past her as she slowed, unsure where to go.

"How can I forget a white jeep, not to mention the way you got out of it and approached me?"

"How'd I approach you?" he asked, glancing back at her.

"How did you approach me," she exclaimed with a laugh.

"Yeah, how?" he repeated, smiling as they came upon his light blue rented Toyota Camry.

"Like you were God's gift to women," she said, getting in the passenger seat as he opened the door for her.

"So that's why you came out your face like that?" he asked, looking down at her as he held the door open.

"Maybe," she answered, smiling up at him.

"You shouldn't judge a book by its cover," he said with a smile, then closed the door, walked around to the driver's side, and got in.

CHAPTER 14

He took her around the projects, blowing his horn as he passed Tubah and the others on 7th Avenue. Passing the Cool-out and Fourth Street parks, he explained to her what went on each, from the drugs to the summer league games. Then they went through the block, which was bustling with activity despite the cold January weather, where he stopped and got out to speak with Blass for few minutes. Next, he drove past Memorial Field, where football games were played and concerts were sometime held. He circled around through Wilson Woods, which was where barbecues were held and the kids went swimming during the summer. While driving through the north side, which he told her they called The Heights, they passed nice homes with well-kept lawns and cars in the driveways. He even showed her Mount Vernon High School, which he had been kicked out of.

"Now the next time somebody tells you they're from Mount Vernon, you can say, 'I know where that's at'," he said, coming to a stoplight.

"This can't be the grand tour 'cause I still haven't seen where you live," she replied, frowning over at him.

"I didn't want you to think that was the reason I brought you up here," he said, playing it safe.

"Well, was it?" she inquired playfully, peering over at him.

"No, of course not," he answered, pretending to be offended.

"That's good to know, but I would really like to know where you live since you know where I live."

"That's not a problem," he answered, making a right off Lincoln and turning down Columbus, while hoping his aunt wasn't home. A thought that made him realize he needed his own place.

Parking across the street from his building, he glanced up at the windows of the apartment to see if any of the lights were on. Fortunately, nobody was home. Getting out of the car, they went into the building and up to his apartment.

"This is where I live with my aunt and younger cousin," he said, shutting the door behind them.

He clicked on a light in the hall, then walked into the living room and turned on a lamp.

"Have a seat. You want something to drink?" he asked, passing her as she came in the living room behind him and he made his way to the kitchen.

"Yeah, whatever you got, as long as it's not alcohol," she yelled to him, while removing her coat and laying it on a chair as she sat down.

"Ain't no alcohol in here. Besides, all I drink is Heinekens and champagne once in a blue moon," he said, returning with two bottles of papaya juice and handing her one as he took a seat next to her.

"Well, I'm just making sure," she replied, taking a sip of papaya.

"It's hot in here," he said, coming out of his sweatshirt.

"So how come you haven't asked me if I have a man?"

"Truthfully, 'cause I don't care."

"Well, excuse me, but why don't you care?" Ameina asked.

"Because I'm not looking for nothing serious, and if you had something serious, you wouldn't be here."

"Mmm, how old are you?"

"I just turned eighteen."

"You're kind of deep for a young motherfucker," she remarked, smiling at him.

"Why, how old are you?"

"I'm a young twenty-two," she answered with a smirk.

CHAPTER 15

"The lawyers said now that the dude you beat up is out of critical condition, he can get you out on bail," Kamari explained to Big Mike, who sat across from him in the visiting room.

"Yo, K, man, what happened?" he asked, staring at him with puffy bloodshot eyes from too little sleep and too much crying.

He had been messed up emotionally since hearing of Darlene's death. The fact that she was fucking his so-called man when killed didn't even fit into his understanding of what happened. All he knew was that she was dead, and he wanted to know why.

"Big Mike, this ain't the time or place. When you get home, we'll talk. For now, just get yourself together," he said, taking in the shape he was in. "Did you have any idea that she was cheating on you with that nigga?" he asked, trying to make him understand that the bitch wasn't worth his grief.

"Huh?" Big Mike said, as if he didn't hear the question.

"I asked you, did you have any idea that she was fucking Vic?" he repeated, using Vic's name as a way of getting some type of response.

71

"No, man, no," he answered, denying the truth of it more so than answering the question.

"Yo, you gonna be a'ight. You'll be home in a couple of days. When you get there, you just have to stay busy to keep your mind off of things."

"I wanna go to the funeral," he blurted out, not hearing the rest of what Kamari said. "Do you think the lawyer can get me out before the funeral?"

"I don't know, but I'll ask him," he said, thinking to himself that it wouldn't be a good idea with the way Big Mike was acting.

"Yeah, I'm gonna call him when I get back upstairs, but you talk to him, too. I know you can make it happen, K. That's what you do, make things happen," he said, speaking rapidly, trying to convince Kamari.

"Don't worry, I'm on it," Kamari said, getting up to leave. "A couple of days and you'll be home, a couple of days," he repeated, embracing him before turning to leave.

CHAPTER 16

"What the fuck you mean nobody gets something for nothing?" Kamari said, twisting up his mouth at Ameina, who was sitting at the table with him inside Sammy's Seafood Restaurant at City Island in the Bronx.

"I'm saying, I could do bad by myself. What I need a nigga for if he can't do nothing for me?"

"Good thing you got that nigga downtown, because you'll be doing bad waiting for me to do something for you," he said with a smile, referring to some dude out of Harlem she told him she was talking to.

"He gives me what I want, and I give him what he wants, if I'm not busy," she added, smiling. "Fair exchange ain't robbery," she added, putting a fried shrimp in her mouth.

"So what am I getting for those shrimps?"

"My time," she replied, and they both laughed.

Ameina was upfront and direct, much like him in a way. She let him know from the jump what she was about, telling him the night they were at his aunt's apartment what she expected in any relationship with a man, serious or otherwise. Kamari listened as she talked about her last serious relationship, which was with Rome. He still had not told her about the night he came to Rome's apartment with Chew and seen her. One day he would, he told himself. The chemistry was there between them, but neither was yet willing to compromise their principles. It was a challenge he welcomed, having summarized the only meaningful relationship they could have was sexual.

"You think highly of yourself," he stated, then took a sip of his strawberry daiquiri.

"If I don't, who will?"

"You'll never know if you keep placing material value on yourself, instead of letting someone who really cares about you show you how much you mean to them through action."

"Maybe you'll be the one to show me since you're so deep," she said, winking as she smiled over at him.

CHAPTER 17

It was 11:25 p.m., and Big Mike stood alone at the bus stop near Valhalla Jail waiting on the last bus to Yonkers. His lawyer had brought up the money given to him by Kamari so that he could post his own bail, but he had not waited to give him a lift home. Darlene's funeral had been held the previous day, and missing it only added to his depression over her death.

Turning up his collar in an effort to keep the cold wind from blowing down his neck, he looked down the dark road and saw the bus coming. Stopping in front of him, the bus doors opened, and he got on, paid his fare, and proceeded to the back, which was nearly empty at that late hour. Sitting down, he made himself comfortable for the long ride home. As he sat there, he thought about what he was going to do once he got there, when the thought occurred that he didn't know what he was going to do without Darlene. He was going to find out from Kamari what happened, who killed his girl, his beautiful Darlene.

"She was so beautiful," he whispered as he drifted off to sleep, dreaming that Darlene was still alive, and she loved him, only him. He smiled in his sleep at the serenity of his dream.

"Hey, buddy, this is the last stop," said the bus driver, tapping him on the shoulder.

"Huh...huh?" he grumbled, awaking with a flash of anger toward the man standing before him, who was responsible for pulling him away from his dream back to his nightmarish reality.

Seeing the look on Big Mike's face, the bus driver took a step back.

"Look, I don't want any trouble," exclaimed the bus driver as Big Mike got up and exited the bus onto Yonkers' Getty Square, which was almost deserted. The public timepiece in The Square showed it was a quarter after midnight, but Big Mike was not concerned with the time as he began to walk in the direction of School Street. As he got a couple of blocks away from The Square, Mink rolled up on a silver and black Ninja 750.

"Yo, Big Mike," Mink called out to him, without removing his helmet.

"Yo, who's that?" he asked, as he stopped and turned in his direction.

"K sent me to get you," he answered.

"Oh yeah, I need to talk to him," he said, coming toward Mink.

As he got to within inches of him, Mink pulled out his .357 and shot him four times in the chest. The slugs ripped holes in his back as they exited, and he fell to the ground. Popping a wheelie, Mink took off down the street, bending the corner, leaving Big Mike's body sprawled out on the curb with a puddle of blood forming around him.

Kamari had found out from Big Mike's lawyer, who had spoken to the prosecutor, that the dude Big Mike had beaten with the bat said Big Mike had did what he'd done to him because he was sleeping with his girl, Darlene. If Big Mike had lied to him about that, then what else had he lied about, Kamari asked himself, and set out to answer just that, which turned out to be an answer not difficult to find.

Come to find out everybody knew Vic was fucking Darlene, Big Mike included. Word was Darlene was like a bitch in heat and Big Mike knew it, but was sprung. So, he tried to beat off the dogs instead of leaving the bitch alone. Then he found out that his man Vic was fucking her, too, but he was locked up by then, and Vic was not the type to be easily scared off. He had to find another way to deal with him, so he kept quiet about it until he did. His chance came when Vic kept asking him to plug him into Kamari, which he had told him no at first because he knew he couldn't be trusted.

77

However, after finding out he was fucking his girl, he agreed, telling him that he would have to pay for his attorney, which was only to make the 360° turnaround look legit. He put him onto Kamari knowing that he would fuck up, and sure enough, he beat him for ten thousand in work and cash. Then, to add injury to insult, he hit him over the head and took his jeep. Therefore, Kamari took Vic out of the picture for him, just as he planned so he could have Darlene all to himself. What he wasn't counting on was two things happening, though. One, Darlene would be with Vic when he told Kamari where he could find him, and two, Kamari would find out how he played him like a pawn. However, he did.

CHAPTER 18

Kamari jumped out of the new Jeep Cherokee Wagoner he purchased to replace the one taken by Vic. This one was champagne gold. Making his way up to the front door of Erica's house, he noticed a candy-apple red Honda Accord in the driveway. He had called before coming, so she left the door open. Going upstairs, he found her in the kitchen, dressed in slippers, shorts, and a Boston College t-shirt, putting something in the refrigerator. She had not heard him come in, and as she closed the refrigerator door, he walked up behind her and took her in his arms.

"Kamari, don't do that! You scared me half to death," she exclaimed, breaking away and turning to face him with a hand over her chest.

He smiled at her as she stood before him, her face bright with the glow of youth and the beauty of a woman.

"I'm sorry," he apologized, taking her in his arms again and kissing her on the forehead. "But you knew I was coming. So, you should've known it was me," he added, taking a seat at the kitchen table as she went to the sink to wash a plate she had been eating from off of. "Whose car is in the driveway?"

"Mine. My father gave it to me for my birthday," Erica answered, placing the plate in the dish rack and drying her hands.

"He getting it like that," he replied jokingly.

"It's not new; it's used," she said, coming over and sitting on his lap.

"Well, I've got a birthday gift for you, too," he said, while smiling and reaching into the pocket of his jacket.

"What is it?" she asked, returning a smile.

"Happy birthday," he said, handing her a small velvet jewelry box.

"Thank you," she said, taking and opening it.

Inside was a white gold rose in half bloom encrusted in diamonds, an addition to the charm bracelet he had given her for Christmas.

"Oh, it's so cute, Kamari. Thank you," she said excitedly, kissing him. "But why a rose?" she asked, remembering how he had explained the meaning behind every charm.

He had said the teddy bear symbolized the comfort he found in her, the butterfly was for her free spirit, and the heart represented the goodness she possessed within her.

"Well, your birthday was yesterday, and with age comes change. That's what the rose symbolizes...your bloom into womanhood."

"Awww... that's so sweet," she whimpered, planting kisses all over his face, and ending with a passionate kiss that led to him carrying her to her bedroom he introduced her to some of the pleasures of womanhood doing things to her, he'd never done before.

Following the session in her room, Erica got up and went into the bathroom where she prepared a bubble bath for them.

"Come on, the water is ready," she yelled, sticking her head through the bedroom door and then disappearing into the bathroom.

Climbing out of the bed, in the nude, Kamari went after her. When he reached the bathroom, she was already in the tub, her head the only part visible in the bubble-filled tub.

"What if your mother comes home and catches us?" he asked, joining her in the tub.

81

"We'd have to get married," she answered, laughing.

"Yeah, a'ight," he said, slinging suds at her.

"Why didn't you ask that question when we were in my room doing the nasty?"

"The nasty, huh? I ain't heard that in awhile," he replied with a laugh. "Because I was too busy to think about anything but what I was doing."

"Oh, so you need something to do. Is that what you're saying?" she came back with a grin, while moving over to him so she could straddle his thighs and face him with her breasts in his face.

"Yeah, I think that's what it is," he answered, placing his hands around her waist, as she took hold of his erection, raised up with some help from him, and guided him inside of her.

"Shhh... Haaa..." she breathed, placing her hands on his chest, while slowly lowering herself and taking the full-length of him inside of her.

Leaning forward, she kissed him as she began to move in an up-and-down motion. Sitting up, Kamari caressed her back and took her breasts in his mouth. As she continued to ride him, the water added to the friction, bringing him closer and closer to releasing.

When they finally got out of the tub, Erica laid in her bed and admiringly watched Kamari as he dressed. After he left, she remained in bed, basking in the afterglow of their lovemaking until she drifted off to sleep.

CHAPTER 19

The incident with Big Mike had left Kamari with a bad taste in his mouth. It was his first taste of betrayal, and he didn't like it at all. It had cost him to bring Mink in to put a wrap on the whole thing, unlike before, when Blass had been shot. Then, he had convinced them that it was in their best interest to get involved being that it had interfered with him moving their coke. So, he provided the guns and they took care of it. Now without Big Mike, Yonkers was no longer an outlet for distribution, so he was sitting on excess coke. All of this was on his mind, as he stood posted up in front of Shabazz with Mink, Dave, and Joel on a brisk winter evening.

Down towards Big Al's, a few dudes from Lindsay's crew were horsing around and throwing snowballs at each other, which wouldn't be going on if Lindsay was around. When Kamari was down with them, Lindsay used to stress that playing on the block or in public makes you seem vulnerable and weak to your enemies. This one thing that Kamari had learned from Lindsay stuck with him, and he preached it adamantly to his own crew.

"It's supposed to snow again later," remarked Blass in reference to a statement from Joel about the weather.

"Yeah, well, somebody's enjoying it," Kamari said with a nod toward the snowball fight going on down by Al's, as

Shonda, Jackie, and Brenda were coming up the block. They stopped in front of Al's to avoid being hit and waited impatiently for the dudes to stop throwing them back and forth so they could pass. Mink watched as Shonda and her girls came up on him, Kamari and the others.

"Where you heading?" he asked when they reached them.

"Shit, I didn't think I was going to make it with them fools throwing snowballs like they crazy," she said, while standing before him in the bell-cut mink coat he gave her for Christmas. "What's up, Kamari?" she added in the same breath.

"What's up, Shonda?" he replied, smiling at how fast the words came out her mouth.

"Where is it that you ain't think you was gonna make it?" Mink asked, rephrasing his original question.

"Tammy's baby shower. I told you about it two days ago."

"Yeah, well, I forget shit that got to do with babies," he said, while shrugging his shoulders and making Blass and Joel laugh, as Kamari looked on smiling and Dave remained stone-faced.

"Let me get out of here. You get around your friends and start showing your ass, and I'm not even about to feed into the bullshit, Mink."

"Yeah, I know one thing, you better be home when I call," he yelled, as they continued up Third.

"Whatever, Mink," she yelled, without looking back.

"Let me find out you tryna lock a female down," said Kamari, staring at him with arched brows.

"What, nigga? You know I don't give a fuck if a bitch run off to Mexico. I just get tired of hearing her telling me I act like I don't care, so I do bullshit like this, and she's happy," he explained straight-faced.

"Yeah, I bet you call later to make sure she's home, nigga."

"Yeah, I gotta do that to make it look official."

"Yeah right, nigga," Kamari replied with a smirk, as Sonia drove by and blew her horn, which he acknowledged with a wave.

"Yo, what's up with Chew?" asked Blass.

"He's a'ight. They doing their thing out in DC. He be coming up, but they don't be staying long," answered Kamari, while reaching for his beeper that was vibrating on his hip.

Looking at the screen, he walked over to the block phone that was on the corner where they stood. After dropping the necessary coins into the phone, he dialed Amiena's number.

"What's up?" he said when she picked up.

"Damn, that was quick," she said jokingly.

"Everything's a game with you," he said, before hanging up and walking back over to where Mink and them stood.

He wasn't in the mood for games, and with Amiena, everything was a game. He'd been dealing with her for almost a month now, and he had yet to get her into bed, which probably had to do with the fact that he was unwilling to spend money on her other than to take her out to eat. True, he wanted to know her sexually, but he was beginning to question if it was worth the effort.

CHAPTER 20

Kamari left the block a little before eleven o'clock and went down to his aunt's on 2nd Street, where he called Tasheeva who had beeped him minutes earlier. Monique was pregnant and getting married to some professional athlete, and they wanted him to come out to the wedding. He declined not feeling it appropriate after what they shared, but promised to send a gift. Afterward, he headed out to New Rochelle to pick up some money from Grant. On his way home, Amiena beeped him again, some 3-1/2 hours after he had hung up on her. He thought about just going home and not returning her call, but chose instead to pull over at a phone booth on Lincoln Avenue just inside of Mount Vernon.

"Yeah," he said, hearing her say his name as she picked up.

"Why don't you come over? I want to see you," she said sweetly, getting to the point.

"See me about what?" he replied, sounding disinterested.

Sucking her teeth, she said, "Why don't you come over and find out."

"Look, I'm not tryna come all the way out there for nothing."

"Oh, that's how you feel? I'm nothing now."

88

He didn't respond right away. This was the first time he ever heard her talk like this, so he didn't know if she was playing another one of her games or what.

"A'ight, I'm on my way," he finally answered, then hung up.

CHAPTER 21

By the time he arrived at her apartment, it was well after midnight. She opened the door wearing a peach-colored chemise, with slits up the sides and that hung just low enough to cover her buttocks. On her feet, she wore a pair of red slippers. Her hair was pulled back into a ponytail, and her makeup-less face exuded such natural beauty that her dark-skinned ancestors had to be smiling proudly down upon her.

"Where is your mother?" Kamari asked as he entered.

"She went with her church on a bus trip to Atlantic City," she answered.

Closing the door, she beckoned him to follow her through the apartment, which had most of the lights out.

"They gambling in the church now," he replied, his eyes glued to the sultry movements of her calves, hips, and firm behind as she led the way to her bedroom.

"Bingo," she answered, as if bingo was not a form of gambling.

Her bedroom seemed to have everything in it you would find in an apartment. There was a 32-inch color TV and VCR on top of a five-drawer, cream-colored bureau with brass handles, which sat in the right corner a few feet from the bottom end of her queen size brass bed. On the left side opposite the bed sat a stereo system beside a smaller matching vanity bureau, which held all kinds of perfumes, body moisturizing kits, and jewelry. The speakers to the stereo were located in the corners on the same side, and on the other side of the vanity bureau was a mini fridge. There were clothes, some with tags still on them, hanging from racks mounted on the wall above each speaker, and stacked up against the wall below them were boxes of shoes. Despite all of this, her bedroom, which was painted French pink, didn't appear crowded. Everything was neatly placed, giving it a comfortable feel.

"Give me your coat," she said, turning toward him as they came to a stop in the center of her room.

"You have everything in here except a stove," he commented, smiling as he handed over his Woolridge.

"I like to have everything I need within my reach," she replied, as she hung his coat up in a closet behind the bedroom door.

"Well, it looks like you accomplished that," he said, glancing around the room.

"Yeah, for now, now that you're here," she responded, walking up and kissing him on the chin as she reached down to undo his belt buckle.

"Oh, you need me," he replied unconvinced, while gently taking hold of her by the shoulders as he stared down at her.

"Yes, right now. I need you badly," she whispered, stressing the word 'badly', as she completed the task of undoing his pants.

She then began running her hands up under his shirt, caressing his chest. Helping her fulfill her needs, he removed his shirt and the thermal he wore under it.

"Get undress," she said, slowly pulling away and moving over to the stereo, as he sat on the bed and took off his boots.

Ameina inserted a cassette in the tape deck and pressed play before turning around to face him. By now, he sat stock naked on her bed, with his arousal drawing her eyes' attention. After stepping out of her slippers, she slid the straps of her chemise off her shoulders, letting it drop to the floor as Ready for the World's "Let Me Love You Down" began playing through the speakers. Kamari stared in awe at her body, which at 5'7" was a work of erotic art, as she stood before him in only a pair of peach-colored lace panties. Her dark skin shined radiantly as she moved toward him with her breasts and their mocha areolas defying gravity. Reaching him, she stood between his legs and placed her arms around his neck, while looking down into his eyes.

"Is this what you wanted?" she whispered.

"Isn't this what any nigga would want?" he answered, putting his hands on her hips and hooking the sides of her panties with his fingers.

He then slowly slid them over her hips and down her thighs to her knees before she assisted him by stepping out of them. Standing up, he took her by the waist and spun her around on the bed, where she landed on her back and spread her legs invitingly while staring up at him. Kneeling between her legs, he took her left leg, placed it over his right shoulder, and began running his tongue down her calves to the insides of her thighs, where he directed his attention to the pink folds of her pussy.

"That's it," she exhaled in a voice heavy with lust, while he flicked his tongue over her pleasure bud.

He remained between her legs until they trembled. Not able to take anymore, she pulled him up. Lying above her with his hands planted on the bed, he stared down into her face, which held a blissful smile from the aftershocks of his oral performance. Reaching down, he took hold of his manhood and entered her. Having reached her climatic heights, compliments of his tongue, her response was less than enthusiastic as he moved up and down inside of her. When he finally reached his peak, he pulled out and rolled over onto his back.

"Pass me that," she said drowsily, pointing to a towel that sat folded on the vanity bureau stool.

Swinging his feet off the side of the bed, he got up to get the towel, retrieving his boxers as he returned to the bed, and handed it to her. Sitting on the side of the bed after putting on his boxers, he glanced back at her as she wiped herself off and spoke what was on his mind.

"Yo, you know what? Your shit wasn't all that," he said, recalling all the shit she talked since he met her.

"Ah, ah... no you didn't, nigga. Your shit wasn't all that," she retorted, hitting him in the back as they both began to laugh.

He was laughing at her reaction to his honesty, and she was laughing because in a way, he was right. She had put little, if any, effort into pleasing him after he'd serviced her, but that he would have the nerve to say what he said both amused and embarrassed her. All the times she had used dudes for her own sexual pleasures, none had ever said such a thing.

CHAPTER 22

On line at the drive-thru of Kentucky Fried Chicken on Boston Road and Baychester in the Bronx, Kamari was in the drivers' seat of Joel's topless white with beige interior Sahara Jeep Wrangler, with his sister Dahlia and their cousin Leslie, who was the same age as Dahlia. Things were back on track, going for him as he felt they should be. The rest of the winter had passed without incident, and the spring of '88 came in with him enjoying the independence and luxuries afforded him through his dealings of drugs. He moved out of his aunt Stacy's apartment into his own place in New Rochelle, which was in the name of another one of his aunts.

In the hood, his name was ringing, which brought both negatives and positives. The positives were dudes wanted to get on his team because they knew he was about his business. Females also kept their ears to the streets just as much, if not more, than the fellas, which allowed him to pull females on the strength of his name alone, with little, if any, conversation. The negative was that always hearing his name and seeing him ascend in the game at such a young age ignited jealousy in some who were older and had been in the game long before him, but were not yet on his level. The thing that made jealousy so dangerous was that it was an unpredictable and sometimes unforeseeable emotion that sprung up where you least expected it. It wasn't so much that they were doing wrong; it's just that Kamari was doing right.

In the game, you're only as good as your connect, and Kamari had a great connect, with others trying to solicit his business.

Oscar had told his father's friend, who he was working for, about Kamari and he wanted to meet him. However, Kamari was not interested, because he had Marco's people who delivered to his front door at a good price for no extra cost. Then there was Ameina's cousin who wanted to meet him.

Ameina even redeemed herself after a less than stellar performance their first time together. His comment about her not being all that had put her on a mission to prove otherwise, and prove it she did. The next time they got together, she was the aggressor, undressing him at the door, giving him head, and displaying the full range of her sexual skills, which was anything but average. They began to compete with each other sexually in bed, with her getting the best of him more often than not. She had a talent she learned from an older cousin, in which she would squeeze the walls of her pussy around him, forcing him to climax even when he didn't want to. He never complimented her on her skills, but there was no need to since his response in bed said it well. He even gave in and started buying her gifts, such as earrings for her birthday, a cocktail ring here, and some Gucci bags there. She stopped seeing the kid from Harlem, even though Kamari had made no commitment to her. Her reason for doing so, as she said, was that he had become a pest, always calling and wanting to see her. Kamari didn't care one way or the other, because after Natasha he didn't trust any female enough to get involved with one seriously.

"Welcome to Kentucky Fried Chicken, may I take your order?" a female's voice blared through the intercom system when they finally reached it.

"Yeah, let me get a four-piece hot and spicy, all breast, with coleslaw and a large cola," yelled Kamari, while leaning out the window.

"Will that be all?" asked the female.

"Nah, hold up." He turned to Dahlia, who was sitting beside him in the passenger seat. "What y'all want?"

"Get me the same thing, but no hot and spicy and coleslaw," said Dahlia.

"Yeah, me, too," added Leslie from the backseat.

"Give me two more four-pieces, all breast, regular, no coleslaw with two large cola. You get that?"

"Yes, will that be it?"

"Yeah, that's it," confirmed Kamari.

"Please pull up to the window for your order."

"Y'all better check your shit, and make sure you got what you ordered," he said, after paying for and receiving their order. "A'ight, we straight," he said, nodding at the cashier, who smiled at him as he took a bite of chicken.

He then pulled out onto Boston Road and turned onto Baychester. He drove enjoying the beautiful spring day as the wind blew wildly through the topless jeep, messing up his sister and cousin's hair. He made a right onto Nereid in the direction of Mount St. Michael's all-boys Catholic school, and popped in a Doug E. Fresh cassette. He turned up the volume as "Keep Rising to the Top" pumped through the 15-inch speakers in the back. Continuing down Nereid, which was a quiet residential section of the East Bronx near Mount Vernon, he made a right at Mount St. Michael's School. Up ahead, a car was double-parked, blocking his path. However, he was not about to stop. Stepping on the gas, he went into the opposite lane and around the parked car, forcing oncoming traffic to stop in order to avoid crashing into him, as his sister and cousin screamed while gripping the crash bars. The oncoming cars blew their horns angrily at him. He cleared the double-parked car and whipped the jeep back into the correct lane in time to spot a detective car amongst the oncoming traffic. Glancing back, he could see them making a U-turn to come after him. Dahlia and Leslie had noticed them, also, and watched as they made their U-turn in pursuit of them.

"Bruv, you better pull over," Dahlia said, looking back worriedly.

"Nah, fuck that. They're Bronx cops; they can't come in Mount Vernon," he replied, turning down the music.

Making the left up Pittman, which changed into Sanford Boulevard, he entered Mount Vernon. Driving past 10th and 9th Avenues, he turned up 8th, where he came to a stop at a light on 5th Street. Looking through the rearview mirror, he thought he lost them, until he saw the detective car drive pass Sanford, back up, and turn up 8th after him.

"Bruv, here they come," said Dahlia, with a voice that said 'I told you to pullover'.

"What the fuck they doing coming in Mount Vernon?" he cursed as the light turned green and he pulled over, getting out of the jeep as the detectives pulled up behind him. "Yo, what's up? How y'all gonna come in Mount Vernon?" he asked, holding his arms out for emphasis, while smiling at the two casually dressed white men who exited the car.

"The feds can go anywhere," replied the driver nonchalantly, walking toward him as his partner came from around the car to join him.

"Ah shit," exclaimed Kamari, twisting up his mouth and dropping his arms.

"Ah shit is right," said the driver, passing him as he walked up to the driver side of the jeep and removed the keys from the ignition. "You wouldn't happen to have a license to drive like that, would you?" he asked, facing Kamari.

"Nah," he answered.

"Do you have a license at all?"

"Yeah, but I don't have it with me," he replied.

"I figured as much. Did you girls know this guy's not even qualified to drive like that? In fact, he might not be qualified to drive at all," said the driver jokingly, as he turned toward Dahlia and Leslie in the jeep, who responded only by smiling.

"Come on, that's my little sister and cousin. They trust me," said Kamari with a smile.

"You're driving like a maniac with your sister and cousin in the car?" said the other agent, who was now standing on the passenger side door next to Dahlia.

"Hell, it's a nice day. I was just enjoying the weather, that's all. It won't happen again."

101

"I did hear that the weather can have a strange effect on young people. So, we're going to let you slide this time. What do you think about that, partner?"

"We can do that. Besides, we don't build tickets."

"Okay, you get a break, but for future reference, if you can't handle a nice day, stay in the house because someone can get hurt like that," he said, tossing him the keys and returning to his car with his partner.

Kamari watched them back onto 5th Street and head in the opposite direction before he climbed in the jeep and pulled off without a care in the world.

CHAPTER 23

"So what do you think?" asked Marco, as him and Kamari walked down Mount Vernon Avenue with P.R.

"I don't know. It don't look like much is happening around here," Kamari replied, looking at what was the Spanish section of Mount Vernon.

One of his aunts had recently moved into the neighborhood, and on occasion when he'd visit, P.R. would try to convince him to put work out there with him. Marco, who was half-Spanish, was familiar with the area and a few of its occupants, so he was there to give input.

"That's what's good about it. Nobody standing on the corners, so it looks like nothing is going on, but that's not the case," replied Marco. "They conduct their business indoors."

"That's right. There is money to be made, and with a steady supply of good product, who knows," added P.R.

"A'ight, I'ma leave something at my aunt's for you tomorrow. You can pick it up in the afternoon. It's a 70/30 split on trial basis, and 60/40 if I like how things go," Kamari said, coming to a stop in the middle of the block.

"That's cool with me," answered P.R., giving him and Marco five on it.

"We'll see you later then," said Kamari, as he and Marco turned and headed back up the block toward the building his aunt lived in.

If things worked out with P.R., that would make three new acquisitions to his team. The other two being a kid named Low from 115th and Lexington in Harlem, who sold powdered coke and crack around there for him, and a kid named Cush from around 241st in the Bronx, who was moving coke down in North Carolina.

As Kamari and Marco reached the front of his aunt's building, his beeper went off. Looking at the unfamiliar number on the display screen with a 212 area code, he motioned to Marco to continue with him to the phone up ahead on the corner. Dialing the number, he listened as a dude answered on the first ring.

"Who's this?" asked Kamari, with a puzzled expression on his face.

"Yo, Kamari, this is Ameina's cousin Faison," said a male voice, rushing his words.

"Who?" Kamari asked, slightly raising his voice.

"Faison… Ameina's cousin. Hold on, I'm going to get her on the three-way," he quickly replied as the line went silent.

"What's up?" asked Marco.

"It's Ameina's cousin. Fuck, I told her I wasn't trying to meet nobody," he said angrily.

"Yo, Kamari, here she is. Ameina," said her cousin, coming back on the line with her.

"Kamari, this is my cousin, the one I told you wanted to meet you," she began, sounding awkward in the position of middleman.

"Yeah, bee, I heard a lot of good things about you," cut in her cousin, as the operator came on the line requesting another deposit to continue the call, but Kamari didn't want to continue the call, so he allowed it to be terminated.

"What happened?" asked Marco, when Kamari hung up the phone.

"The time ran out," he said, making Marco laugh as they started toward his aunt's. "Wait until I see her later," he added, getting angry as he thought about her lack of regard for what he'd told her.

CHAPTER 24

Chew arrived in New York from D.C. on a Friday. He beeped Kamari that same night around 11:45 p.m., and they made plans to meet in front of the S&S afterhours spot in Harlem. Kamari pulled up on the corner of 145th and 8 th, which was crowded from Willie's Burgers up to the front of the S&S on both sides of the street. Most of the people had come over from the Roof-Top, which had not too long ago let out. Dudes stood posted up with their crews, big jewels dangling from their necks, wrists, and fingers, Cars and trucks sat double- parked, waxed, and Armor All'ed down. Each crew was made up of mostly dealers getting money somewhere in Harlem or the Bronx. Then there were the females who came from all over that stood in their little groups, either mingling with them or just admiring them from a distance.

Kamari spotted Chew, who signaled to him from where he stood with his god-brother and a few other dudes. After double-parking his jeep in front of Chew's god-brother's white 325 BMW convertible, he got out.

Chew, who was an inch shorter than Kamari at 5-foot-nine, had a slim build, with skin the color of ginger. He wore his head balled in total contrast to the fro he had the last time Kamari had seen him. He was wearing a pair of Polo denim jeans and white Polo sneakers, with a white and black

106

Harlem USA T-shirt. He smiled broadly as Kamari approach him in a cream Christian Dior velour sweat suit, with cranberry stripes down the sides, and a pair of white on white Nike Cortez.

"What's up with the ball head?" Kamari joked, as they embraced.

"The fro is a dead giveaway that you're from New York and D.C.," he answered, smiling.

"So what you saying, being from New York is a crime out there?"

"Damn near."

"Well, why don't you stay your ass home?"

"Two words: the money," he said with a smirk.

"Yeah, that's always a good reason," he came back.

"You should come out there and see what kind of money I'm talking about," said Chew.

"Maybe one day I will," Kamari replied, nodding to Chew's god-brother, who stood a few feet away from them talking to a slim, dark- skinned, pretty-boy type in a Yankee cap, who was one of Harlem's own.

In the hood, most dudes were known by the cars they drove, and then there were those who switched rides so much you couldn't keep up with them. So, you identified them from the blocks they hustled on or the crews they ran with. Then there were those who got money from so many different blocks and didn't deal with just one crew. This type of dude would be known by name, and you would always hear his name because people would always be talking about him. This was how legends were made in the hood, which was the category of the dude who Chew's god-brother was talking to fell in. He was a legend in the making.

"What's been happening with you?" said Chew.

"I'm progressing, so I can't complain."

"Yo, Chew, what you going to do? Want to shoot over to a pool party in Jersey?" asked his god-brother, while coming over to where they stood.

"I'm cool. I'ma chill with Kamari. You go ahead. I'll see you tomorrow."

"A'ight," he said, making his way to his red 325 BMW convertible, as the slim dark-skinned kid climbed in the black one parked behind him and pulled off first with him following behind.

"I ain't with being all up in those niggas' faces. Let's go get something to eat," Chew said, while talking to Kamari but watching as a brown- skinned female passed them dressed like Janet Jackson in the Control video from the black jeans and T-shirt to the hairdo.

"A'ight, where you wanna go?"

"Let's go over to the steakhouse on 86th Street," Chew answered, as they made their way over to Kamari's jeep.

CHAPTER 25

The steakhouse was located on Third Avenue between 86th and 87th next to a movie theater. Patrons usually caught a movie and then came in for a late dinner of grilled steak prepared to order.

Kamari and Chew had about a 20-minute wait after placing their orders before they were ready. They took their orders to the upstairs dining area, which was less crowded than the lower level where people sat to in order to be seen or to see who came in and with whom. Toward the back, they sat at a corner table that afforded them the maximum view of their surroundings.

"Does Sonya know you back?" Kamari asked, looking up from the task of buttering his baked potato.

"Nah, I'ma go check for her tomorrow."

"How long y'all staying?"

"Until Sunday, as it stands now, but ain't no telling?" he answered, digging into his steak.

"You remember that female your cousin was messing with...Ameina?"

"Yeah, what about her?"

"I ran into her and bagged her."

"You fucking her!" Chew half-shouted, arching his brows and smiling.

Kamari just smiled back in response.

"She's about that paper, nigga. That's all she fucks with is niggas getting it," he continued when Kamari didn't answer.

"Yeah, I know. She don't have a problem letting a nigga know either," he answered, grinning.

"Yeah, well, I would give her a G or two to hit it if it was that simple, but with females like her it's never simple."

"Yeah, she's anything but simple," Kamari replied with a smirk, recalling how she had given it to him half-ass for free.

They talked about what was going on with everybody since the last time they spoke. After finishing their meals, Chew decided he wanted to see Sonya and called to let her know he was coming over. Kamari dropped him off and went through the block before heading out to his place, where Shelly was waiting on him. He had gotten accustomed to taking Erica, Shelly, and Ameina to his apartment. However, out of the three, only Erica and Shelly he would leave alone while he went out to handle business, knowing that they would not answer his phone. Ameina, however, was a different story. Though their relationship was supposed to be one of no attachments, she had too much shit with her to be trusted.

CHAPTER 26

"You got this nigga, right?" asked Tubah, helping Moose into a pair of 13- ounce black boxing gloves.

"Yo, I told you I got this," answered Moose, while scratching his nose with his gloved right hand and glancing over at his opponent, who was a kid called Skinny from 70 projects.

Not only was he skinny, as his nickname indicated, but he was also tall. At 6'4", he had Moose by three inches, not to mention the reach advantage. Moose was put together physically, though. Outweighing Skinny by ten pounds, he was known for being agile and good with his hands. Therefore, when he and Skinny started arguing about something stupid it was time to break out the gloves, which was a common practice in the hood for settling disputes amongst friends.

"A'ight, I'ma put two-hundred on you," said Tubah, sounding convinced.

"I know one thing, get knocked out if you wanna by that boney motherfucker, and you better not show your face around here no more," interrupted Mink, who stood with Kamari, Dave, and several other dudes out in front of Ebony Gardens on Seventh Avenue, placing bets on the hood-promoted fight.

113

"If Skinny knocks my ass out, I'm going down South to stay with my grandparents and become a farmer," replied Moose, throwing a series of combinations to get loose.

"A'ight, that's what I'm talkin' about. I got five-hundred on Moose. Who likes Skinny?" shouted Kamari, holding his money in the air.

"I like my nigga Skinny. What up?" said a stocky kid named Myles, who ran with Skinny.

"I told you what's up. All you gotta do is call it," Kamari replied, turning toward him.

"The five is called," Myles said, as Skinny walked up beside him. "Let's get it on then," he added, putting a hand on Skinny's shoulder and smiling.

Moose and Skinny moved into the middle of the street to square off, with everyone whooping, hollering, and gathering around them in a circle. Skinny had a simple style. He stood with his guards held high in front of his face, with no movement of the head or anything. Moose was the total opposite. His stance was more conventional as he bobbed his head from side to side, talking trash, faking jabs, and trying to get a feel of where Skinny's heart was at. Skinny just stood there not intimidated, staring across at him, and only moving to keep Moose in front of him. Stepping inside,

Moose threw the left jab, but before his arm was fully extended, Skinny backed him up with two sharp right jabs to the face.

"Bob and weave, nigga," yelled Tubah. "Bob and weave…"

Hearing him, Moose regrouped and went back in, standing straight up. However, this time when Skinny parked the jab, Moose got low and caught him with two body- curling blows to the midsection.

"Yeah, that's what it's about, nigga. That's money right there," shouted Tubah, cheering him on.

"Yo, traffic!" shouted someone from the crowd, and the two fighters broke to let the traffic through.

"What are you boys doing out there?" yelled the nosey old woman from the window of her second-floor apartment in Ebony Gardens.

"Nothing, Ms. Wilson, we just sparring with the gloves," replied Tubah.

"All right now, y'all be careful," she said, remaining in the window as Skinny and Moose went at it again in the street.

Skinny was making things difficult for Moose with his jab. Realizing that he might have to take one to give one, Moose got more aggressive working the body. Skinny tried to adjust by coming down on him with the overhand left, but he didn't have much effect on him due to the body blows Moose was landing almost at will.

"It don't look go for you, boy," said Kamari, smiling at Myles.

Skinny's jab had lost all of its snap, and Moose began to toy with him by standing straight up, ducking and weaving everything he threw, and talking mucho trash as he did so. Both of them were dripping with sweat, but Moose's sweat might as well have been cold water, because he looked fresh, unlike Skinny who was stumbling on wobbly legs. Taking advantage, Moose stepped in and threw a three-piece left jab, right overhand, and left uppercut that put Skinny on his ass.

"Yeah, motherfuckers," Tubah yelled, throwing his arms up as he ran over to Moose and scooped him up in the air. "And the winner is Too Loose Moose!"

"Meet me at old man Capp's later, and I'll give you a chance to win your money back," Kamari said, accepting his winnings from Myles.

"I ain't fucking with you, nigga. If you serious about letting a nigga get some back, the gloves is right here," he challenged, looking Kamari in the face with a tight smile.

116

"What ! You can't be serious," exclaimed Kamari, looking at him like he was crazy.

"Why ain't I?"

"A'ight, but I can't come out of character for no punk-ass five-hundred," he said, glancing at Mink who stood beside him with Dave, as Tubah and Moose came over.

"Make it a thousand then. I don't give a fuck."

"Make it ten thousand 'cause I do give a fuck," Kamari replied, his face expressionless.

Myles didn't respond; he just stared angrily back at him.

"I'll rep that G spot for Kamari," shouted Knox, who had been in the cut with Stan listening to the conversation. Together, he and Stan made their way over to the crowd. "That's if it's all right with you, Kamari?"

"I don't have a problem with it, if it's all right with him," Kamari replied, looking from Knox to Myles, who both had similar builds.

This was the second time in less than five minutes that Kamari had put Myles on the spot. Myles didn't have ten thousand dollars, but he'd be damned if he was going to have niggas thinking he didn't have any heart neither.

117

"Let's do it," Myles said, turning and walking over to Skinny, who was still recovering from the beating Moose put on him, to get the gloves.

"What's up, nigga?" said Mink, grinning at Knox.

"I'm about to show you," he replied, returning his grin as he took the gloves from Moose.

"Yo, I got a little thirty dollars. Can I get a bet on my man?" shouted Stan, money in hand, as he spun around glancing at the crowd.

"Yeah, right here. What's thirty ones?" said a kid from the projects, knowing he was betting on a long shot.

Knox had been hanging up in the Vernon on the regular, and niggas heard about, if not seen, his knuckle game. Only a few was in his league, and Myles was not one of them.

Knox stepped out into the street in his trademark all-black tank top, sweats, and Reebok classics. This time, unlike when Moose and Skinny went at it, there was no rooting or side-betting going on. Niggas was just waiting to see what they knew would be the outcome, and the ones who didn't know were waiting to find out if what they'd heard about the kid from Brooklyn was true.

Myles stepped out in front of Knox and put up his hands. Knox smiled a sinister smile, the one he had flashed Kamari at the party the first time he had seen him, and put his guards up. Myles threw a jab with his left and that was it. Knox stepped outside Myles's lead foot and slid forward so that his head was at the elbow of his extended jab. Then he came with a crushing overhand right that landed smack on Myles's jaw. His head jolted back on an angle, as his knees gave out under him, and he went down, knocked out cold.

"Damn," Kamari said, turning to Mink who was smiling.

"I know, that was fast," replied Mink.

"Shit, *he's* fast," Kamari responded, as Knox came over to them while removing the gloves. "Yo, you're really good with those things, huh, kid?" he said when Knox reached them.

"Where I come from you have to be good or get use to watching a lot of TV," said Knox with a smirk.

"Here you go, Kamari," said Skinny, breaking in and handing him the thousand dollars.

"A'ight," he replied with a nod, taking it. "Yo, here," he said, turning and handing it to Knox.

"All of it?"

119

"Yeah, it was your hustle, and besides, you hit that nigga so hard you might have to cop a vest," he said, laughing.

"Keep talking like that and I'll have to come back and finish what I started," Knox replied, and they all started laughing.

"Nah, you good. If anything, he's heated with me."

"Yo, I've been wanting to get with you on something," Knox said, changing the subject.

"Yeah? Well, walk with me to my jeep, and I'll give you my number so we can hook up. Excuse us for a minute, y'all," he said, as him and Knox made their way over to his jeep.

Opening the passenger door, he sat down with his feet on the curb, and then removed a piece of paper and a pen from the glove compartment.

"Here you go," he said, writing down his beeper number and handing it to him.

"Yo, you doing your thing out here, and me, I'm tired of the stickup thing. I'm trying to get some real money. I notice how Mink came up fucking with you, so is there a spot for me on your team or what?"

"Yo, just call me. We can do something if you're for real."

120

"Yo, I'm for real," he said, as Ameina pulled up on the corner in the gold Benz with her girlfriend.

Kamari watched as she got out and walked over to them, her hips rocking under the white Gucci tennis skirt set she wore, with the sneakers to match. The whole block watched as the dark-skinned beauty ascended on Kamari, who could tell she was enjoying the attention by the sly little smirk on her face as she made eye contact with him.

"Yo, I'ma talk with you later," Knox said, about to walk away.

"Nah, it's cool. Don't go nowhere," he said, getting up and leaving the jeep door open, as he went to meet her on the sidewalk.

Feeling comfortable with Kamari, Knox took up position in the passenger seat.

"What's up with you giving some nigga the number to my beeper?" Kamari asked when he reached her.

"It wasn't some nigga. It was my cousin, and I didn't give him your number. I beeped you and put his number in," she answered, standing before him.

"I don't give a fuck who it was. I don't know him, and didn't I tell you that I didn't want to meet nobody?"

"I know. I told him you were going to be mad, but he kept buggin' me," she explained.

"So the fuck what," he said angrily, raising his voice.

"I know I shouldn't have done it. I'm sorry."

"Shit," he exclaimed for lack of anything else to say. "So what you doing up here anyway?"

"Don't worry, I ain't come up here to cause no trouble for you with your local girlfriends," she replied, smiling.

"Go 'head with the bullshit. What you want?"

"I need some money to go out."

"Here," he said, handing her some money.

"What am I suppose to do with fifty dollars," she complained, staring at the money in her hand.

"I don't know. Where you gonna hang out at, Vegas?"

"Come on now, I can't do nothing with this," she replied, holding it out to him.

"Well, give it back then," he said, reaching for it.

"A'ight, give me fifty more," she bargained, pulling her hand back quickly.

"I shouldn't give you shit for not listening to me," he said, while peeling off another twenty-five and handing it to her.

"I said I was sorry," she replied, taking the money.

"And bring me back something from wherever it is you're going."

"What? With seventy-five dollars? You gots to be joking," she exclaimed, turning to walk away.

"I ain't playing. Come here," he called out, trying to keep a straight face.

"What?" she whined, then stopped and came back as he walked up to her. "What?" she repeated, as he took her by the arm, pulling her to him and whispering something in her ear that made her laugh. "Yeah, right," she teased, smiling and walking away.

Grinning, Kamari turned and headed back over to Knox, who had been watching the whole exchange.

"Yo, I ain't tryna be nosey and shit, but what you whisper to her?" asked Knox, as Kamari looked at him and smiled before answering his nosey question.

"I told her that she got out that Benz like she was God's gift to men," he said, still smiling.

"Oh," replied Knox, not getting it, which made Kamari laugh.

CHAPTER 27

Together at the place he shared with his sister, Mink and Shonda lay in bed, breathing heavily as beads of perspiration glistened on their bodies, a telltale sign of the intense sex they'd just finished sharing. Now the intense silence that followed weighed heavy in the room, as did the thoughts that consumed them and kept them from falling to sleep.

Mink's inability to fall asleep not only had to do with what was on his mind, but also with the fact that he was high on cocaine. He'd started using the stuff a couple of months ago one night when he was out alone at Wally's Strip Club and one of the strippers passed him a bill of coke. Instantly, he liked the euphoric feeling it gave, taking his mind off the things he had been struggling to push from his thoughts lately. One of which was the death of Staggs, whose loss he had never really grieved, but as time passed, the lack of his presence kept impeding on Mink's conscious and emotional resolve. Then there was Dave, who was no longer Dave, which was a painful reminder of the post-Staggs era in which their friendship now existed. It was like being around a stranger who looked like his friend. Dave showed no enthusiasm or emotion for life. He didn't want to hangout anymore, preferring instead to spend time with Candy, the female who lived on his block. He didn't even speak unless spoken to, and even then, he said very little. His sister had even inquired to Mink as to what was wrong with her brother, for which he had no answer. Mink missed the comradery of Staggs and Dave. He felt like a loner. Having never learned to express his feelings while growing up, he kept it all buried inside. Now it was beginning to overflow, and with cocaine, he had found a way to contain it.

Shonda's thoughts were as hectic as those of the young man in whose arms she laid with her head resting on his chest. She ran her fingers along the scars on the right side of his chest, reminiscing about the night he'd been shot and what she felt being there with him. She recalled seeing him get shot, staring down at him covered in blood, his blood on her hands, and the feeling of losing something she'd never really knew but longed to know with her entire being. Lying with him now, she knew with certainty at her young age of nineteen that she'd never felt so close to anyone as she did Mink, and never would. Knowing this, she did not understand why she was so afraid to tell him that she was pregnant with his child. Most men who lived the type of life he lived dropped their seed off in any female willing to spread her legs for them, but not Mink. From what little she learned from his sister, she figured it had something to do with his father dying when he was very young. She knew he cared for, if not loved, her because he done things with and for her that he had never done for any female. His friends even teased her, asking what she had done to him. A question that always made her feel good.

Yeah, girl, you're in love, she told herself, smiling.

Then it came to her why she was afraid to tell him, and her smile faded. Though all she wanted was to know him, she was no closer to knowing him now than she was the day she met him. That's why she was afraid to tell him, because she didn't know him well enough to know what his reaction would be. It would hurt her deeply if she told him and he were to tell her to get rid of it. She might even be so hurt that she would do it out of anger. She wasn't going to let that happen, though. The doctor told her she was two months pregnant, so she'd wait until it was too late for an abortion before telling him. Whatever came after that she'd just have to deal with, because she felt her life would never be complete without Mink or a part of him in it.

"Shonda?" Mink called out softly.

"Huh?" she answered.

"You still up, too, huh?"

"Yeah, just thinking."

"About what?"

"Life," she said, closing her eyes.

CHAPTER 28

"I have to stop off at my cousin's," Ameina said, climbing into Kamari's jeep as he picked her up from in front of her building.

They were going out to catch a movie and then retire to his place for the evening.

"What for?" he asked, watching as she placed a brown bag between her feet.

"His nurse didn't come in today, so I'm taking him something to eat and make sure he's all right."

"Where at?" he said, pulling off.

"Lakeview, 106 and Madison."

Ten minutes later, they came to a stop in front of the Lakeview housing projects. Kamari shut off the engine and sat back in his seat. "Hurry up," he said, exhaling his displeasure with having to delay his plans, which were plans he made to please, because he didn't even like the movies.

"You don't have to sit out here. Come on up," she said, staring across at him.

"I don't wanna go up. Just hurry up."

"Stop acting like that," she cried, pausing as she continued to stare at him. "Come on, Kamari, 'cause I might be a minute," she added pleadingly.

"A'ight, what the fuck," he relented, opening the door and getting out, figuring he'd go ahead, meet her cousin, and get it over with so they'd leave him alone.

CHAPTER 29

On the ninth floor, her cousin unlocked his apartment door after buzzing them up. Kamari followed Ameina inside, closing the door behind them. At a glass table in the dining room, her cousin Faison sat in a wheelchair. He was a couple of shades lighter than Ameina, with thick eyebrows. He wore his hair in a natural curly low-cut Afro, with a neatly trimmed mustache that adorned a pair of wide flat lips. Dressed in gray sweats and a V-neck t-shirt with socks on his motionless feet, he looked like help was the last thing he needed, as he sat there sporting a gold watch with diamonds in the face and a big doorknob gold ring covered in diamonds on his pinky. He had an extremely vibrant look for someone in a wheelchair, Kamari thought in his assessment of him.

Walking over to him, Ameina set the bag of food on the table, then leaned over and kissed him on the cheek.

"Thanks, Mena," he said, as she turned and went to the kitchen. "Damn, man, I finally get to meet you," he said, smiling charismatically up at Kamari, who remained standing by the door, and without giving him a chance to respond, Faison continued. "I heard a lot of good things about you, you know. Not just from, Mena, but a few dudes I know up your way. They say you're a laid back, keep to yourself, kinda dude, who don't really fuck with a lot of niggas," he said, pausing. "So, I understand you not wanting to meet me," he rambled on, as Ameina came and took the bag of food to the kitchen to heat it up.

"Nah, it ain't like that. I got my niggas who I fuck with, who are mostly dudes I came up with, ex-car thieves and burglars turned drug dealers, and I'm comfortable with that," Kamari explained, as Ameina returned and placed a plate of hot food in front of Faison, along with a glass of water.

He thanked her before she departed to the living room, which was adjacent to the dining room. Kamari watched her take a seat on a brown leather couch and pick up a magazine to read, which confirmed to him that his being there was planned.

"Please, have a seat, Kamari. That is, if you don't mind sparing a few more minutes of your time. I'm just glad for this chance to meet you," he smiled, pointing to a chair in front of him on the other side of the table.

Accepting his offer, Kamari sat down.

"See, what you just said confirms everything I heard about you. You have good qualities for a dude your age." His smile was now one of admiration. "It's like this here, bee; I don't want nothing from you. I got some people you might want to deal with for product."

131

"I'm good with the people I deal with," Kamari said, cutting him off.

"Yeah," he responded, pausing. "What are they charging you?" When Kamari didn't answer, he continued, "If you don't mind me asking."

"Sixteen a brick."

"That's damn good, but how is it?"

"It's moving without complaints."

"Mmm, yeah, at sixteen that's $2,000 an eighth. I tell you what, why don't you try an eighth of what my peoples got. I can get it for you at the same price, and if it's better and you like it, we can work something out," he said, staring across at Kamari as he waited for an answer.

"We can do that," Kamari said, already anticipating the outcome, but not wanting to close any doors in other areas.

"Tomorrow. Then I'll have it for you, and just get back to me from there," he said, extending his hand to Kamari, who stood to shake it.

They exchanged numbers, and Kamari left with Ameina, not really knowing what to think of the dude he had just met in the wheelchair. True, he was a smooth character, but that was a common trait for most dudes from Harlem with a little money. The question was could he be trusted, and if so, in what way could he be of use to him.

CHAPTER 30

On the Deegan Expressway, Kamari drove downtown accompanied by Knox. They had been spending a lot of time together as of late, which Kamari used to get to know the kid from Brooklyn. Kamari had never really passed judgment on him, something for which he was glad of now that he had taken the opportunity to get to know him. Knox was honest and upfront, always saying what was on his mind, characteristics one wouldn't expect to find in a stickup kid from Brooklyn.

The first time him and Kamari hooked up after his knocking out of Myles on Seventh Avenue, he looked Kamari in the eyes and said, "You know what? When I first started coming out here," he paused for a second, "I was going to get you."

Kamari had just laughed at his boldness and told him he must have planned not to come back to the Vernon. Then he asked him what made him change his mind. To which Knox answered that after being out on the block and observing the way he moved, he began to develop a respect for him, because although Kamari had weapons and was getting money, he remained the same, never changing in the people he dealt with or how he dealt with them. He never wore big jewelry or made a spectacle of himself. Knox said that most dudes who are robbed be asking for it, but that wasn't the case with Kamari and he respected him for that. He went on to tell Kamari about moving to Brooklyn from England when he was very young and being teased, beat up, and robbed on the streets of Brownsville by other kids because of the way he talked or for whatever other reason would serve their purpose. Eventually, he learned to defend himself, becoming the aggressor, the predator, and making others his prey. Kamari related this to his experience at Robert Fulton, only not as severe. However, it made him wonder if his situation had been as bad, would he still be the person he was today, would he be like Knox, or would he even had made it this far. He was glad he had not passed judgment.

Turning off the Deegan at the 155th Street Bridge exit, the traffic was somewhat heavy as they moved across the bridge at a slow pace. One of the many crack heads that cleaned car windows for change came up to Kamari's jeep on the driver side.

"Yo, don't put that dirty rag on my windshield. I'm good," Kamari yelled out to him, while rolling down his window, but he sprayed water on his windshield anyway and began wiping.

"What the fuck, are you deaf or something?" shouted Knox, as he jumped out of the jeep on the middle of the bridge and moved around the front end of the jeep to the vagrant drug addict, who was trying to wipe away the water he'd sprayed on the windshield. "Are you hardheaded or stupid?" sneered Knox, reaching the man.

As the filthy dressed crack head in rags finished wiping away the water, he turned toward Knox to say something, but never got a chance to get it out. Knox punched him in the face, knocking him out stiff as a board.

"Yo, Knox, what the fuck is you doing? Let's go," yelled Kamari, looking down at the man stretched out along the front end of the jeep, as Knox climbed back in the passenger seat. "Yo, you a crazy motherfucker," he said, shaking his head as he pulled off.

CHAPTER 31

Knox waited in the jeep while Kamari went up to Faison's to meet with him about the cocaine he'd gotten from him a couple of days ago. He'd put it up in New Rochelle with Grant, telling him that it was a different product and to let him know how it was compared to the usual product. When he reached his apartment, an older woman opened the door, leading him in. He assumed she was Faison's part- time nurse. Faison was sitting at the table like before in his wheelchair and pajamas and a robe, as Kamari walked over and took a seat across from him. The nurse disappeared into a room in the back, leaving them alone to discuss business.

"So how was it?" asked Faison, eager to see where he stood.

"It was good, but not better than the stuff I'm getting'" he answered, using Grant's words to him.

"Yeah," he said, pausing. "So who's your peoples?" he continued with a laugh, to which Kamari responded by flashing him a smile. "Look, you don't have to tell me," he added, smiling.

"Some Colombians," he said with a shrug, as if it was nothing.

"Well, I hope we don't become strangers, you know. Let's get together sometime and hangout. Go out to eat, whatever, you know," he said genuinely.

"Yeah, we can do that. You got my number," he answered, as he stood to leave.

"Okay, then, I'll be in touch," Faison replied, as they shook hands and Kamari left.

CHAPTER 32

From inside the shower, Kamari thought he heard his phone ringing. Sticking his head outside the shower curtain, he listened for it to ring again, but there was only silence. He had a busy day ahead of him. There was a scheduled appointment with his probation officer, and Cush, who he had to get up with, was flying in from North Carolina this afternoon. Faison, who he had been dealing with on a social level, hanging out in Harlem, meeting females and dudes out there, and eating at all the hotspots in Manhattan, wanted him to come and check out the possibility of opening a spot on 129th Street. He also had to call Marco's people and arrange to re-up before week's end.

Stepping out of the shower and drying off, he wrapped a towel around his waist and walked across the hall to his bedroom. His room was simply furnished with a dresser, two nightstands, a television and VCR on a stand at the foot of the bed, and a full-length mirror on the closet door. He was proud of his one-bedroom apartment, which his aunt Stacey helped him to furnish. Aside from the bathroom, bedroom, and kitchen, there was a drop-floor living room covered with a thick off-white carpet, and which was anything but simply furnished. With its low to the floor, deep-cushioned, mahogany-colored leather couches and chairs, the living room gave one the illusion of sinking when they entered and sat down. There were matching mahogany tables with almond lacquer tops and a 42-inch color TV and VCR on the wall, along with a sound system. He had an assortment of old black exploitation movies from the 70's that included *Cornbread Earl, Claudian, Cooley High, Cross 110th Street,* and his two favorites *Black Caesar* and *Hell Up in Harlem.* He tried to collect them all.

Just about everyone in the apartment building where he lived in New Rochelle worked during the day, so they hardly ever saw him leaving, and by the time he came in at night, they were all asleep. He didn't keep any drugs in his apartment, only a small safe and a .380 Beretta that he sometimes carried on him.

As he stood up to put on his jeans, the phone rang. He picked it up from the nightstand and sat down on the bed.

"Yeah, what's up?" he said into the receiver.

"What are you doing?" asked Erica.

"Getting dressed," he answered, putting on his jeans. "Did you call here a few minutes ago?"

"No, why?"

"Nah, I thought I heard the phone ringing while I was in the shower."

140

"Well, it wasn't me," she said, implying something else.

"So what's up?" he asked, ignoring the undertone of her remark.

"You," she replied, not letting go of whatever it was bothering her.

"A'ight, that's cool, but besides me. What's happening with you?"

"What," she exclaimed, feigning excitement. "The way they've been talking about you lately I didn't think there was a *besides* you," she said sarcastically.

"Look, why don't you just say what's on your mind so we can deal with it and move on," he said, waiting for her response.

"You have another girl, don't you?" she said, like it was something she already knew.

"Come on now, why you say that?" he asked, thinking one of her friends might have seen him with Ameina.

"Girls talk, Kamari."

"I got nine aunts and four sisters, but did you know that they also lie?"

"So do y'all," she came back.

"Yeah, but not as good as y'all, and I know ain't no female tell you that she fucks with me," he replied, knowing that he hadn't been dealing with any females in the Vernon lately other than her.

"I'm asking you do you have another girl? And you don't have to lie to me neither, Kamari."

"No, I don't have no other girl," he answered, knowing he could never tell her anything that would hurt her, even if she asked him to as she had just done.

Besides, he wasn't claiming anyone. So, to him, it wasn't exactly a lie.

They stayed on the phone a few minutes longer making plans to get together later before hanging up.

CHAPTER 33

With all the day's events behind him, Kamari's day was now winding down. As he pulled up in front of his aunt's on Mount Vernon Avenue, Marco and Oscar were waiting on him. Jumping out of the jeep, he went upstairs where his aunt opened the door for him, saying that P.R. gave her some money to give to him. Walking into the smoke-hazed living room, he found Marco and Oscar kicked back smoking weed.

"Fuck, why don't y'all open a window in this motherfucker?" he said, doing just that before taking a seat, as his aunt came in carrying a joint of her own and handing him the money P.R. left for him.

"Yo, bee, chill. I got the crazy deal for you from mi jefe," declared Oscar, sitting up on the edge of the couch.

"Yo, Marco, what the fuck is he talking about?" Kamari asked, thinking it was the weed talking.

"Let him tell you. It's his deal," replied Marco, taking a pull from his joint.

"Yo, come on, bee. I'm serious," Oscar said defensively.

"A'ight, I'm listening," said Kamari, staring over at him.

"I can get you consignment on whatever you buy," he declared with a smile.

"What do you mean on whatever I buy?"

"I mean, however many keys you buy, he'll match on consignment, if you want to take them."

"So if I cop two, I leave with four and bring the money back for the second two when I return."

"That's right, and here's the catch. After the first time, you can get them all on consignment, no money needed," said Oscar, smiling with half- closed eyelids.

"How much for a brick?" Kamari asked, thinking there had to be a catch.

"Eighteen, which is two more than you're paying now, and the same quality."

"On both, what I pay for up front and what he gives me on consignment?" Kamari asked, still skeptical of the whole thing.

"Yo, bee, he wants to meet you first so you can work that out with him," stated Oscar.

"Why he wanna give me such a sweet deal?"

"Because I told him about you, and this is how they deal amongst each other. You're my man, so they're going to deal with you like you're one of their own. And with all the coke they have, they can do whatever."

"Yo, Marco, what do you think?"

"You gotta do what's best for you. Yeah, my people are going to be mad, but if they can't come better, then fuck it," he answered, reading Kamari's mind.

"A'ight, so when does he want to meet?" Kamari asked, looking from Marco to Oscar.

"I'm staying up here tonight, so we can go out to Queens tomorrow and do it."

"A'ight, how about I pick you up tomorrow afternoon?" Kamari proposed.

"That'll work," Oscar said, sitting back on the couch.

They sat around discussing the Columbian drug trade and its two cartels, the Medellin and Cali, the latter being that which the guy Kamari was going to meet tomorrow was associated with.

CHAPTER 34

On the drive out to Queens, Oscar filled Kamari in on what would be expected of him before a deal went down from his boss, whose name was Elias and who spoke no English. Fortunately, Oscar would be able to translate everything Elias would say to Kamari.

In the Jackson Heights section of Queens, they pulled onto a side street off Northern Boulevard, where a payphone was located out front of a small grocery store, and exited the car. Kamari stood by while Oscar beeped Elias and punched in the number of the payphone, along with a code so he would know it was him.

"It shouldn't take long for him to call back," said Oscar, hanging up.

"Yeah, a'ight, I'ma go get something to drank. You want something?" Kamari asked, heading for the store.

"Yeah, bee, get me a soda and some barbecue chips," he answered, standing by the phone so that no one would use it.

Inside the store, Kamari brought a cran-apple juice and bag of onion and garlic chips, along with what Oscar wanted.

"Here you go," he said, handing Oscar his soda and chips as the phone began to ring.

"Hola," said Oscar, answering the phone. After speaking a few words in Spanish, he ended the call and turned to Kamari. "Let's go. We have to meet him at his friend's auto body shop," he relayed to Kamari, as they made their way to the jeep. "Here, you drive," said Kamari, handing him the keys.

CHAPTER 35

Less than twenty minutes later, Oscar turned into a fenced-in drive-way alongside a garage that was located on a block that was more industrial than business or residential. The driveway led to the back of the garage, where several late-model American cars were parked. Standing in front of a midnight blue '84 Caprice classic were two Columbian men, both short in height. One was dressed in dirty overalls, and the other, whom Kamari figured to be Elias, was casually dressed in tan slacks, a white button-up short sleeve shirt designed with palm trees, and a pair of brown leather moccasins with white soles. At about 5'5", he had skin the color of weak tea, with thin black hair that he wore laid down on top of his head. His eyes were dark and Mongolian in characteristic, with the rest of his facial features falling in line with that of a South American Indian. Despite his height, he had a unique and imposing look, sort of like Genghis Khan. Kamari guessed him to be in his early to mid-30's, as Oscar parked alongside the Caprice and they got out. "Como estan," shouted Oscar, as they approached.

"Bien y tu," replied the man Kamari pegged to be Elias.

"Bien, bien." Oscar then introduced Kamari to the casually dressed man, as the other man said something in Spanish and walked to the garage.

"Como usted. Mi nombre es Elias," he replied, extending his hand with a smile, which Kamari accepted. "Tu eres policia, " he continued, while still holding Kamari's hand as he stared up at him.

"What?" Kamari said with a frown, catching the police part before Oscar could translate.

"He asked are you police," translated Oscar, smiling at him as he stood there clasping Elias's hand.

"Tell him I am only eighteen. How I'mma be the police?" he responded without looking away from Elias, who remained clutching his hand.

Oscar translated what Kamari said with a laugh, to which Elias replied with something else in Spanish as he released his hand and broke into a smile.

"He said, you never know," repeated Oscar in English.

"Yeah, he's right about that," Kamari said with a smirk, as Oscar translated it to Elias.

Oscar and Elias continued to speak briefly in Spanish before Oscar relayed to Kamari what was being said. He told Kamari to leave his jeep behind, and that they were going to take the Caprice up to Kamari's apartment in New Rochelle and discuss business while they drove. Leaving his jeep

149

behind, he climbed into the back of the Caprice, while Elias sat up front with Oscar, who drove. On the ride up to New Rochelle, Elias told Kamari that he should have no problem selling a lot of cocaine because he spoke English.

"Yeah, imagine if I spoke Spanish, too," replied Kamari, with Oscar translating.

"No te preoccupies, tu tiene a Oscar para eso," responded Elias, smiling.

"He said, don't worry. You have me for that," relayed Oscar, glancing back at him.

One at Kamari's apartment, Elias walked around inspecting every room before they sat down to hammer out the terms under which they would be doing business. Elias had wanted eighteen a key for both those paid for up front and those taken on consignment, which to Kamari was not acceptable.

Finally, they met halfway at seventeen up front and eighteen on consignment. Elias explained to Kamari that the faster he moved them the more he could get. Whatever he could handle would be his limit. In other words, he was saying the game was the same on every level; it was all about the flip. Don't sit on it.

When they returned to the garage, Kamari shook hands with Elias on a deal set for the next day, with two keys paid for in

150

cash up front and two on consignment. Oscar would pick him up and take him to do the transaction, at which time he would take a cab back. With the deal concluded, Kamari jumped in his jeep, feeling good about the connect he'd just acquired, and headed for Harlem to put the second part of the plan he'd worked out in his head the night before into effect.

CHAPTER 36

Faison sat at his dining room table listening as Kamari sat opposite him, offering him a partnership he could not refuse. "As of tomorrow, I'ma be getting bricks from a new connect on consignment for eighteen a brick. His main thing is how fast I can move them; that's what he wants to see," Kamari explained, pausing as he stared across at Faison, who nodded for him to continue. "The faster I move them the more I get. I want you to get down with me on selling weight to the niggas in Harlem and elsewhere."

"How much are you looking to get for a brick?"

"Twenty at the least."

"That ain't much of a profit at eighteen a brick," Faison remarked, raising his brows.

"I know, but check it out. Let me tell you what was told to me. You have two cartels in Colombia that control the majority of the drug trade over here. The Medellin and Cali cartels have a man placed in various cities across the country. Now let's say they have a man in New York, and the price of shipping keys to him from Columbia to Miami to New York is five thousand a key. Their man here has his people who he gives these keys to on consignment for ten thousand dollars a key, and they sell them at whatever price they want so long as the man gets his ten. You see, that's where we're at. We're one man away from the man who represents the Cali cartel here in New York. Anything over ten is a profit for our man, so if we can move ten bricks or more every week, I can get him to come down."

"I thought you were dealing with Colombians already?" replied Faison.

"I was, but they're down on the totem pole. They can't supply a demand for ten or better, and definitely not on consignment. With this new connect, there's no limit; if we can move it, they can supply it. Look, I'm not asking you to stop your thing you got going. I'll even get your product from the connect if you want. I'm keeping the things I got going on in the Vernon and elsewhere. With cash up front, I'm going to be getting them for seventeen, which is a G more than what I was paying before. But we can use this consignment thing to take it to another level on both ends; mine and yours," he finished, smiling as he thought about the possibilities.

"Now what's my part in this again?" Faison asked, with a wide grin.

"All you gotta do is help move them, and you get fifty percent on every one you move."

"What if someone wants a half a brick?"

"I'd prefer to unload them by the brick, but I'll break them down for $10,500 a half, but nothing smaller."

"How many are you getting tomorrow?"

"Two plus my re-up."

"A'ight, so when do you want me to start putting the word out that I got it?"

"I'll call you tomorrow when the deal is done."

"I ain't going anywhere. I'll be right here waiting," Faison replied, laughing excitedly.

CHAPTER 37

Oscar picked Kamari up in the same Caprice they drove around in the day before. When they reached Queens, they beeped Elias, who immediately called back and told them where to meet him. The meeting spot was in the middle of a block in the Astoria section of Queens, where Elias stood under the shade of a tree with three other Colombian men drinking beer. Parking across the street from them, Kamari and Oscar exited the car and headed over to them.

"Como ellos estan," said Oscar, smiling as they came up on Elias and the men.

"Bien," replied Elias, along with the men.

Turning to one of them, Elias spoke briefly with him, before saying something to Oscar and acknowledging Kamari with a nod. Leading the way to the Caprice, he got in the passenger seat, all the while speaking to Oscar who climbed in behind the wheel. Kamari, who did not understand a lick of Spanish, figured he was telling him where to go as he slid in the back seat.

"Yo, tell him the money is under the seat," said Kamari to Oscar as they pulled off.

"Le dice que solo tengo dos kilos, y que tendre los otros manana," replied Elias, after Oscar translated Kamari's message.

"He only has two keys for now, but he will have the other two for you tomorrow," relayed Oscar to Kamari.

"Whatever, it don't matter," Kamari answered, figuring he had nothing to lose.

He was paying for two bricks, and that's what he was getting. True, it was at a price more than he was use to paying, but if Elias was going to trust him with consignment, he had to show some trust on his end, as well. When Oscar translated Kamari's response, Elias smiled and nodded his head.

Fifteen minutes after picking Elias up, they pulled up in front of a two-story brick home in a residential area. Removing the bag of money from under the seat, Elias got out.

"Vamos," Elias said, as they followed him inside the house they had parked in front of.

Inside the house, there was no furniture. Only curtains covering the windows.

"He never furnishes his apartment because he never stays in one more than three months," explained Oscar, reading the expression on Kamari's face.

"Esperen aqua," said Elias, leaving them standing in what appeared to be a living room, while he disappeared into another part of the house.

He returned minutes later, having removed the money from the bag and replacing it with the two kilos of coke.

"Yo tendre los otros manana para ti," he said, handing Kamari the bag.

"Tomorrow he'll have the rest for you," said Oscar to Kamari, who checked the contents of the bag and nodded his agreement.

Leaving the house, they dropped Kamari off at a Latin-owned taxi stand and saw him safely off in one before departing.

CHAPTER 38

When Kamari went to see Faison and inform him that they'd have to wait another day to get the coke on consignment, he was disappointed and somewhat doubtful of the reality of everything Kamari had told him, which to him sounded too good to be true. However, like Kamari in dealing with Elias, he, too, had nothing to lose in dealing with Kamari regardless of the doubts he held.

"Pull over right there," Kamari said, directing Oscar to a parking space in front of Faison's building in Lakeview. Oscar did as Kamari said and parked the midnight blue Caprice, which now belonged to him, a gift from Elias. With the engine running, Oscar placed the car in neutral, pumped the emergency brake three times, pushed in the lighter, and then ran a coin across the top of the dashboard, releasing a hidden compartment under the dash behind the radio. Removing its contents, he handed it to Kamari before closing it, and they exited the car for the building. Faison, who was expecting them, buzzed them up, and they took the elevator up to his apartment.

"What's up?" Faison said, opening the door for them.

As he turned in his wheelchair and rolled back to the dining room table, Kamari came in, followed by Oscar shutting the door behind him.

158

"This is my man Oscar I told you about," said Kamari, waiting for them to exchange greetings before continuing. "The deal is the same, except now we have three bricks to move instead of two," he said, grinning over at him.

"Get the fuck outta here," exclaimed Faison, smiling broadly.

"Yeah, he gave me an extra one for the inconvenience," Kamari replied, taking a seat. "Here, you can start with this one," he said, placing a gray plastic bag containing a brick of coke on the table in front of him.

"They got it like that, huh?" Faison said, directing the statement to Oscar, who nodded the affirmative with a smile.

CHAPTER 39

The bright morning sun shined through the blinds of Ameina's bedroom window and down on the face of Kamari, waking him. Sitting up, he squinted and then glanced at the time display on the VCR screen, which read 7:20 a.m. Beside him, Ameina laid naked with her back to him, a sheet draped over her as she slept. He smiled to himself as images of their night together filled his head. Images that added to the stiffness of the morning hard-on he awoke with, making him more ready for what he had a mind.

Lifting the sheet, he scooted up behind her until her body's warmth became his and vice versa. Nibbling on the back of her neck, he reached around and caressed between her legs. To this, she responded by mumbling something that was punctuated with a soft moan, making him smile mischievously. Unsure if she was asleep or faking, he took hold of his erect member and proceeded to enter her from behind.

"Mmm…Ahh…," she moaned, waking and turning slowly toward him as he continued to push his way inside of her. "What are you doing?" she asked, a smirk on her face.

"What do it look like I'm doing?" he said with a smile that bordered a laugh, as he leaned over and kissed her on the mouth.

160

"Stop, nasty! We ain't even brush our teeth yet," she protested, frowning.

"So what," he replied, kissing her again.

Giving in, she opened her mouth, allowing him to explore with his tongue as she returned the gesture, and then he began to move slowly inside of her.

"Hold up," she breathed.

Rolling over onto her back, freeing herself from him, she accommodated him by spreading her legs as he moved between them and reentered her. Their bodies moved together slowly at first, then after finding each other's rhythm, their pace increased. Their arousal grew with a jolt of pleasure each time their pelvises met, pushing them closer to their destination. Ameina, despite being awakened from her sleep, gave herself to him with the same vigor as she had done the night before, entwining her legs with his as they climaxed together.

Returning from the bathroom, Kamari smiled down at Ameina, who in his short absence had fallen back asleep. After dressing, he left her apartment and took the elevator down to the lobby. Outside, he couldn't help but smile as the sun beamed down on him in the same manner it had when he had awoke. It was a beautiful spring morning, and everything seemed so alive to him as he made his way to where his jeep was parked, taking in the sights along the way. There was the laughter of children on their way to school, people waiting to catch a bus to work, a stray dog digging in a trashcan, car horns blowing, and the sound of it all played like the theme song to life, his life. Everything was for him on this morning; that's how he felt.

Getting in his jeep, he started the engine and pulled out into the light morning traffic of 2nd Avenue. As he drove in route for home, he popped in his Keith Sweat cassette and turned up the volume, filling the interior with the sound of "How Deep Is Your Love". He was on his way. He had a connect to supply him with as much cocaine as he wanted, and a crew that respected him and moved it for him. He had money, beautiful women to choose from, and his future looked bright.

"So this is what it feels like to be on top," he thought aloud, as he sped uptown on the Deegan, his position in the land of the King now elevated.

CHAPTER 40

Parked out in front of the co-op buildings where Shelly lived in Yonkers, Kamari sat with Marco, waiting on her and Dahlia, who he sent inside to get her. Dahlia, after constantly bugging him, finally got him to keep his promise to take her out with him and Shelly.

"Where was they moving that shit?" Kamari asked Marco, referring to some 90-something grams of heroin Marco gave him two weeks ago.

"I don't know. I told you my people took it from somebody who owed them," he answered, as he reclined back in the passenger seat and stared off in the direction Dahlia would be returning with the female Kamari wanted him to meet.

"Yeah, well, I ask because that brown shit don't sell too good over here. They call it Mexican mud. It sells on the West Coast, but not over here. Over here, it's China white or nothing."

"Fuck I care. Throw it away then," he said, glancing over at Kamari.

"You don't have to tell me. That's exactly what I'ma do if I can't move it," he answered in a matter- of-fact tone. "But talking to this kid Low out in Harlem, I'm looking to get some China white. He said heroin moves like crazy around his way between 115th and 116th on Lexington."

"Yeah, but where you going to get it from?"

"One of my aunts worked in a number spot for this old Italian dude. I hear they be having the connects for it, so I asked her to set up a meeting with him for me."

"Here they come," announced Marco, watching as Dahlia and Shelly made their way to the jeep. "If you never learn how to do nothing else in life, you'd go down as one who knew how to pick 'em," he said.

"Hay, I told you," Kamari replied, as Shelly and Dahlia climbed in the back seat. "What took y'all so long?"

"Shelly, bruh, changing clothes three times and what-not," answered Dahlia, pointing at her accusingly.

"Dahlia, you need to stop it," exclaimed Shelly, smiling over at her.

"Damn, three times for me? That might be a record," said Kamari teasingly.

"Yup, bruh," instigated Dahlia.

"Don't flatter yourself. It wasn't three times. It was twice," Shelly confessed with a smirk.

"Twice? You ain't break no record with that. I think you tied it, though," he said, sounding unimpressed.

"Tied? Tied with who?" she questioned, making them all laugh.

"Nobody. Calm down. I'm just messing with you."

"You can find better ways to mess with me than that," she replied, sucking her teeth.

"Yo go ahead with that," he shot back, smiling over at her. "I want you to meet my man Marco," he added.

"Nice to meet you," she said, extending her hand, all smiles again.

"Same here," said Marco, taking her hand and smiling warmly at her.

"A'ight, where y'all wanna go eat at?" asked Kamari.

"It don't --" began Shelly, when Dahlia cut her off by taking hold of her arm and whispering something in her ear. "How about Red Lobster?" she continued, as Dahlia sat next to her grinning innocently.

"Dahlia, you need to stop hanging around your aunts. This is not a date. I'm your brother."

"It's a date for Shelly," she disputed, making them all laugh as Kamari pulled off.

CHAPTER 41

Through the rearview mirror, Kamari watched as the black Cadillac Allante belonging to the guy his aunt worked for, who every one called Joe, pulled up behind where he sat parked on the corner of Fifth Avenue and Kingsbridge Road in Mount Vernon. Exiting his jeep, Kamari proceeded over to the Cadillac. He could see Joe motioning for him to come around to the passenger side as he approached.

"How you doing? Kamari, right?" asked Joe, with an outstretched hand as Kamari opened the car door and got in.

"Yeah. Joe, right?" he replied, humoring him as he closed the door and shook his hand.

"Yeah...yeah...sure," he said, as they both laughed at the awkwardness of strangers lost in the moment. "Your aunt tells me you wanted to see me, so what can I do for you?"

"Yeah, I guess she told you a little bit about what I'm into."

"Yeah, a small bit," he said, holding up his index finger and thumb for emphasis.

"I sell coke, but I want to do the heroin thing. The only problem with that is I don't have a connect to make it worth my while. You know what I mean?"

"Sure, I know exactly what you mean," he responded with a smile. "How old are you, if you don't mind me asking?"

"I'm eighteen," Kamari answered, wondering what his age had to do with anything.

"Hay, don't take the offensive," Joe interjected, reading the expression on Kamari's face. "You're a young fella, and I just want to give you a little history lesson on things. That way, you'll know a little bit," he said, holding up his fingers again, "about me, and then maybe you can understand where I'm coming from, as well as get a better understanding of what you're into."

"Go ahead, I'm listening," answered Kamari, curious to see where he was going with this.

"I was involved in dealing narcotics in the 70's and early 80's, mostly cocaine. Back then, a key of coke ran you sixty grand, take it or leave it. If you didn't take it, the next guy would. See, what you gotta understand is that we didn't have all the different groups of the South Americans involved in dealing coke back then. It was primarily the Colombians, and they weren't shipping in as much as they are today. That's why the price was so high. Hence the title a rich man's high," he said, pausing. "This created an allure, a mystique for it. If you wasn't doing coke, you were at the bottom of the social ladder, and nobody wanted to be at the bottom. My friends and me made a lot of money back then, which brings us to the present. As all of the other different groups started getting involved in the selling of cocaine, it drove the price down and the drug lost its mystique. When this happened, a few of my friends and me got out of the business, while others switched to heroin. The cocaine business is out of control. There are no principles and too much senseless violence. Any fourteen-year-old kid can go buy a key of cocaine, if he got the money."

"Ain't that the case with any drug?" Kamari said, wishing he could take back his words.

"If that were the case, you wouldn't be sitting here talking to me now."

"So what are you saying?" he asked, all of a sudden feeling hot with anger.

"What I'm saying is this. I'm not into dealing anymore, and all the guys I know who are don't want to meet anyone new. They're old guys, set in their ways and who they deal with. For me, it's numbers. If I get busted, I pay a fine and open up the next day. It's a no-hassle business."

"What was this, your version of a sugar-coated 'no'?" Kamari said, his anger spilling over.

"If that's all you got from it, I'm sorry, because it was a whole lot more there than that," he said, regretfully extending his hand. "It was nice meeting you, and good luck."

"Yeah, thanks for your time," Kamari said halfheartedly, shaking his hand before exiting the car, feeling like he'd just been insulted. *So the coke business lost its mystique now that we're in it, huh,* he angrily thought, as he made his way to his jeep.

CHAPTER 42

"I got two. Who want ounces?" said Blass to Kamari, as they stood in Fourth Street Park with Mink, Knox, Joel, Tubah, and Kamari's cousin Ski from Eighth Avenue, who was the middleman between him and the dudes that had recently started hustling over there.

Kamari had begun selling weight to a few people in the Vernon through his circle, directing them to only deal with those just coming in the game rather than those already knee-deep in it. This way, they established their own clientele. The latter would not cop from him anyway because of the egos, which was cool with him. He didn't want them in his business anyway.

"A'ight, I got you, Blass. What about you, Tubah?" asked Kamari, as he stood in the center of the crowd they formed, with Mink to his right and Knox on his left.

"They'll be ready by the weekend, same as before."

"I got niggas waiting on me right now," declared Joel.

"How many times you gonna tell me that. I heard you the first twenty times," Kamari replied, shaking his head as he glanced over at him. "Ski, what's up with your peoples?" he asked, turning to his cousin who stood next to Mink.

171

Ski was a definition of a pretty boy. He stood 5'9", had a slim build, curly hair, smooth pecan-colored skin, and thick eyebrows that connected lightly over the bridge of his nose.

"Tonight I'ma call and let you know what's up. I ain't seen nobody yet," answered Ski.

"A'ight. What's happening with this game?" Kamari asked, glancing over to the main court where the first game of the summer league tournament was going down between Big Joop's team and some team from the Bronx.

The park was crowded, mostly with locals out to watch the game and enjoy the weather.

"Big Joop's team is getting blown the fuck out of the park," replied Mink, as a tall, cute, copper complexioned female approached, accompanied by a light-skinned female who stood about the same height and was just as cute, if not cuter, depending on one's taste.

She and Kamari had dealt with each other briefly in the past. They had met during his first year of high school. He would go by her house to visit, and she would act like it was all about her. She wanted him to jump through hoops to be with her, maybe because he was younger than she was. Whatever the reason, Kamari wasn't going for it. He stopped going by her house and speaking to her altogether. Then when he started getting money and his name began ringing in the hood, she sent one of her girlfriends, who was messing with his man, to put a word in for her with him. Recognizing it for what it was, he didn't bite. Persistent though, she started bugging his man to the point that Kamari eventually took her out, and what she had wanted him to jump through hoops for a year earlier, she gave to him that night without discussion. She told her girlfriend about it the next day, who said something to Kamari. He responded by saying that he didn't know what she was talking about and that whatever she told her was a lie. In keeping with that, he went back to not speaking to her, as if it really hadn't happened, and she left him alone.

"How you doing, Mink, Kamari, and y'all?" said the copper-skinned female, stopping in front of Mink as the light-skinned girl continued on, telling her friend she'd be waiting up ahead Because she didn't want to be in Kamari's presence.

"Look at you, girl. What are you getting into, besides them jeans?" said Mink, staring down at her behind.

Across from where they stood on the 4th Street side of the park, Shonda sat on one of the benches with Jackie, Brenda, and Tammy, who had her baby boy with her. All their eyes were on Mink and the copper -skinned female, who they knew and didn't like.

Shonda had told Mink about being pregnant and her intentions to have the baby, which didn't sit well with him. They had argued and she refused to get rid of the baby, telling him it was too late and explaining why. Listening to her explain, it sounded to Mink as if she had trapped him. Therefore, everything she said afterward about loving him and the part of him that grew inside of her didn't register.

Observing Shonda, Kamari could see the pained expression on her face as she watched Mink talking and laughing with another female. He also saw the anger on the faces of her girlfriends, and decided he would have to talk with Mink about the situation.

"Yo, could you excuse us? We have some business to discuss," Kamari said, trying to avoid a scene with Shonda and her girlfriends.

"No problem," said the female, smiling. "Mink, we'll talk later," she added, moving on to join her friend in the opposite direction of Shonda and them.

"What the fuck was that about?" asked Mink, twisting up his face at Kamari.

"You know what it's about," he answered, shaking his head.

"Yo, I don't tell you what to do with your bitches, so don't try to tell me what to do with mine," he said angrily.

174

"A'ight, you got that," responded Kamari, knowing that to challenge Mink in front of the others would only make matters worse. His cell phone began ringing, and he answered it. "Yeah… I know…yeah, that's you…a'ight, give me an hour," he said, pressing the disconnect button as he pushed down the antenna. "Yo, I have to shoot downtown. Blass, you gonna take that shit to Less?"

"Yeah, you can give it to me."

"A'ight, Joel, you and Blass follow me. What about to you, Ski?"

"I'ma go check on that right now. I'll get up with you tonight."

"A'ight, then," he replied, giving him five. "Yo, Mink, we gonna hook up later. I need to talk to you about something," he said, letting him know it wasn't over, as they headed to their rides.

CHAPTER 43

Kamari listened to Faison, who sat next to him doing the talking, with Knox riding shotgun as they drove down Eighth Avenue in Harlem. Faison was telling him about a friend of his, a dust dealer in Harlem, who wanted to get involved in the coke game and was in search of a connect. He wanted to set up a meeting with him and Kamari in that regard.

"A'ight, just let me know when," said Kamari, coming to a stop at a light on 135th.

"Hay, pull over right there," said Faison, pointing in the direction of three females coming up the avenue. "Hay, where y'all hookers going?" he called out, as Kamari pulled up alongside of them.

"What?" exclaimed one of the females, while abruptly turning around. "Faison," she shouted in recognition. "Don't even try it, with your big- ass head," she continued, smiling as she came up to the passenger side of the jeep, followed by her two friends.

"Don't take it the wrong way. When I say hookers, I mean it in a good way," he replied, grinning at her as she leaned against the door.

"Yeah, right," they all said doubtfully, twisting up their mouths.

"Seriously," he defended, smiling. "I mean hookahs as in 'so fine a nigga wouldn't mind paying'. Right, y'all?" he said, turning to Kamari and Knox, who smiled in response.

"Don't put them in it," said the dark-skinned, green-eyed female doing all the talking, as she looked from Knox to Kamari.

"Put them in it! Shit, they got eyes. They see the same thing I see, three bad bitches." Reaching through the window, she punched him in the shoulder. "Come on, girl! You got heavy hands."

"Keep it up, Faison. You're pushing it," she warned playfully.

"Where'd you get those green eyes?" asked Kamari, cutting in.

"What?" she said, taken aback by his question.

"The green eyes, where'd you get them?" he repeated, undiscouraged by her response.

"My father, why?" she replied, staring intently at him.

177

"Nah, I've never seen anyone with as rich a skin tone as you with green eyes, and I mean that in a good way," he said with a smile.

"Well, thank you," she replied, returning his smile as Faison looked on.

"Oh, you going for that shit, but when I said the same thing…"

"Shut up, Faison," she said, cutting him off. "You didn't say nothing like that."

Kamari sat smiling at the comical exchange between the two of them, as a car pulled up beside him and blew its horn. Turning, he found himself staring into the face of Ameina, who sat in the passenger seat of her girlfriend's gold 190 Benz staring accusingly up at him.

"What's up?" he said, still smiling.

"What are you doing?" she asked, glancing pass him at the green- eyed female.

"What?" he exclaimed, almost laughing as a car blew its horn behind Ameina, forcing them to pull over in front of him.

Kamari got out and walked over to meet Ameina as she exited the Benz.

"What's up, cousin?" yelled Faison, sticking his head out the window of the jeep as the three females stood looking on.

"Don't cousin me," she yelled back, as she looked up at a smiling Kamari. "What are you smiling at?"

"At you. You should see yourself," he answered, laughing.

"Oh, you think shit is funny. You're not going to be coming out here, being all up in these bitches faces and disrespecting me," she said, getting loud.

"Yo, what are you yelling for? And what the fuck is you talking about?" he replied, laughing the whole time.

"A'ight, play stupid if you wanna. I don't be coming up to where you live talking to niggas in your face."

"I don't know what you be doing, and those are Faison's peoples."

"I know, and I'ma have a talk with him," she said, looking over in his direction. "And what you mean you don't know what I be doing?"

179

"Yo, you buggin'," he said, laughing. "What happened to nothing serious?"

"Yeah, well, shit changes," she replied with a smirk as the females headed up the block, but not before the one with the green eyes yelled out to Kamari.

"Nice meeting you," she said.

At this, Kamari just smiled. Not so much at her, but at the nature of females trying to show up each other.

"See, that's the shit I'm talking about," said Ameina, storming up to the jeep. "Faison, don't be having them bum-ass bitches up his face."

"Hold, cousin, what are you talking about?" he asked, amused by the way she was carrying on.

"I should've never introduced y'all."

"Come on now, Mena, that ain't right. You making something out of nothing. Them girls was talking to me," he explained, sounding hurt.

"Yo, chill, I got this," said Kamari, taking her by the arm and pulling her away, as the ever observant Knox looked on wondering how Kamari put up with the bullshit. "For real, you're making something outta nothing," reasoned Kamari once they reached the Benz.

"No, I'm not. It's something to me. I don't care what you do where you live, but I'll be damned if I let you bring that shit to my doorstep."

"Yo, just go ahead and we'll talk later," he said, lacking the desire to get into a long, drawn-out argument.

"Where you going?" she asked, looking up at him expectantly.

"What?" he said, smiling because she had never asked him that before.

"I asked where you are going. Since you started dealing with my cousin, you barely have time for me anymore."

"I'll come by later," he replied, now understanding her recent actions.

Lately, she had been getting very possessive with him. When he would come to see her, intending only to stay for a few minutes, she would fight with him when he tried to leave, which usually led to some good intense sex in the aftermath. She would say things like she loved him, and he would respond by saying, "I don't love you" with a laugh. To which she would come back with, "You will" with a laugh. He didn't take her serious, though. Her earlier impressions outweighed anything she now did or said, and that combined with what he went through with Natasha was more than enough for him to know to keep his feelings at bay. However, all in all, he found what they had different. Unlike every female he had dealt with before her, she didn't always let him have his way or put her on hold. She fought constantly for him to give her the time she wanted and felt was her right, being she gave him what he wanted when he wanted it. She never told him no, which was the case with most of the females he dealt with in the past. However, unlike them, she wouldn't accept no from him, and for some strange reason, he found that strongly appealing.

CHAPTER 44

Huddled over a bottle of beer at a bar somewhere in Flushing, Queens sat Kamari with Oscar and Elias, as women from some part of South America danced topless on top of the bar. Over the past few months in which Kamari had been dealing with Elias, he had come to respect the little Columbian man, who was his connect. It specked not just from his ability to supply him with cocaine, but also because of the way he and his people moved.

Every transaction was a social one, with dinner, drinks at a bar, or a Columbian Bar-B-Q, all ending with the exchange of cash for cocaine, bringing a touch of class to a dirty and ruthless business. On these occasions, he would also advise Kamari on how to conduct himself. Like once when Kamari and Oscar had stopped off at the Benz dealer on Northern Boulevard after spotting the new 300 Coupe in the showroom window while on their way to meet with Elias, and Oscar told Elias about how Kamari was going to get the new Benz. Elias responded by saying it would not be a good idea. That it would only draw unwanted attention to him and everyone associated with him. Kamari understood, having learned from Oscar, that Elias and his people had been in business for over ten years because of their low profile in the states, sending their money home to Columbia. So, coming from him, Kamari took it for what it was worth and abandoned the idea of a new Benz.

Business also would be conducted with others besides Kamari, all of which would be Colombians, with Kamari being the only exception. This, however, would not always be good business. Kamari would learn this from Oscar, who would always translate to him when they were alone the things that had transpired and the actions that would be taken later in response. Elias had tried to introduce Kamari to this side of his business.

It began with a translation of events from Elias though Oscar. Out in Chicago, which was part of the East Coast network, some individuals had robbed and murdered a few of Elias' people. There was a substantial amount of money being offered to individuals willing to accept a contract on those out in Chicago responsible. Elias asked Kamari if he was interested in fulfilling these contracts. Kamari declined, simply stating that he was a drug dealer and not a killer. To this, Elias had replied with a smile that there was no difference between the two, and that the dealer could not exist for long without becoming the killer.

This Kamari knew, but he also knew that Elias had people who handled such things for him efficiently. Therefore, to bring such an offer to him could only mean one thing. The targets were black and they needed someone black to get to them. He could have easily arranged for Mink and Knox to do it, knowing they would have welcomed the opportunity, and in the process gained himself more favor in the eyes of

Elias and his people. However, he was not about to allow himself to be used in that way. If he did, then he would be no better than the characters he often cursed at while watching *Black Caesar*, who sold their own out to gain favor with the mob back in the 70's. Besides, he knew they would not kill their own if circumstances were reversed. For that reason, his answer had been no. Elias accepted this, assuming that because of his age he had not yet been in a situation where he had to take a life, and with that in mind, he told Kamari that after the first time he did so, the rest would be easy. This Kamari did not agree with, but some things he knew were better left unsaid.

Through his peripheral vision, Kamari noticed someone coming through the front entrance to the right of where they sat. Looking in that direction, he watched as an attractive blonde-haired Columbian woman dressed in stretch blue jeans, a black windbreaker with a pair of white canvas Dex sneakers, and a black purse hanging from her shoulder came toward them. Walking up to Elias, she planted a kiss on his cheek, communicating something to him in Spanish before turning to Oscar, who handed her over the keys to his car. Taking the keys, she departed the same way she came. Kamari started to ask what was up, but took a sip of his beer instead and continued his visual intake of the G-string clad women dancing on the bar in front of him.

185

Minutes after she had left, the blonde woman returned, taking a seat beside Elias and handing him the keys, who in turn handed them back to Oscar with a smile.

"Let's go. We're out of here," said Oscar, standing.

Rising from the bar, Kamari nodded at Elias, who smiled his acknowledgment. Following Oscar, they left Elias at the bar with the woman.

Outside, they made their way to Oscar's car and climbed in. Kamari glanced back at the laundry basket the woman placed on the back seat after removing the money from the trunk. The basket was filled with clothes and a box of Tide detergent, which concealed six bricks of coke.

CHAPTER 45

"How you doing, Ms. Richards?" said Kamari, speaking to his mother's next door neighbor, who was sleeping out front of her house as he exited his jeep.

"I'm fine. What about you? I haven't seen you around lately," she replied, taking a break from her task as he came up on her.

"Nah, you know. I'm just trying to learn how to fly on my own."

"Well, it looks like your soaring like an eagle," she said with a smile, while glancing from him to his jeep.

"I'm doing my best," he replied, as he opened the gate to his mother's home and went inside.

Upstairs in the kitchen, Dahlia was on the phone, while Tia, the second youngest, sat at the table eating homemade French fries prepared by Renée, who was at the stove frying up some more.

"Where's, Ma?" he asked, passing Dahlia and walking up behind Tia, sticking his hand in her plate and taking a few of fries.

"Stop, boy! I don't know where your hands been," she yelled, glancing back at him as he licked his fingers.

"Now you do," he smiled.

"Ma's in her room," answered Renée, glancing over her shoulder at him.

"Bruh, Natasha said hello," called out Dahlia from where she sat on the phone.

"That's who you're talking to?"

"Yeah."

"Give me the phone," he said, taking the phone from her.

He hadn't spoken to her since the day after he put her out his aunt's apartment. Since then, she and Dahlia, who she had taken to like a little sister from the first time they'd met, had grown even closer.

"What's happening with you?" he asked, curious to know how she would respond to him.

"Nothing much. How about yourself?"

"You know me. If I ain't making something happen, I ain't living," he answered, smirking.

Dahlia sucked her teeth as she sat listening.

"Check you out. You need to stop," Natasha replied with a laugh, having had a chance to know a side of him that other females only got a glimpse of, if that.

"Where's your man at?" he asked, referring to some dude Dahlia had told him she was seeing.

"A'ight, bruh, that's enough. Give me the phone," Dahlia said loudly, reaching for it.

"Nah, chill," he said, pulling away. "Yeah, go ahead. I'm here."

"I don't know, probably out with some other girl," she answered, sounding disinterested.

"That's a'ight with you?"

"Hay, what's a girl to do," she responded, the meaning behind her words not lost on him.

"Yeah, well, you know." He paused, trying to find the words to bring the conversation, which was going somewhere he didn't want it to go, to an end.

"Anyway, it was nice talking to you again," she cut in, giving him the out.

189

"Yeah, same here," he said, handing Dahlia back the phone and making his way to his mother's room.

When he reached her room, the door was open. Inside, she sat on her bed engrossed in a book, as his baby sister lay behind her sleeping. Unnoticed, he stood in the doorway keenly aware of her maternal nature as he observed her in her surroundings.

"How long have you been standing there?" she asked, looking up from her book at him, the look of youth still present in her features despite her age and the birth of five children.

"Not long. What's that you're reading?"

"A book by this Jewish woman making the comparison between the slaves that arrived here from Africa and Judaism," she answered, holding the book up for emphasis.

"What's the comparison?" he asked, showing genuine interest.

"She says that the slaves would sing songs of Moses and Pharaoh. They would say to their slave masters that the God of Abraham, Isaac, and Jacob would punish them for what they were doing to them."

190

"That's deep," he replied, understanding a little of what she was saying since they had spoken before about history, psychology, and the Bible.

"They were speaking about you at the temple last week," she said, speaking of the place where she went to study her way of life and worship.

"About me?" he replied with a frown, thinking that nobody at her temple knew him, and hoping that she hadn't been telling them about him.

"About young black men like you. They did a study that shows at the rate young brothers are going to prison that by the year 2000, the amount of young brothers in prison in this country are going to be staggering, and you're falling right into their trap," she said, shaking her head as she stared over at him.

"A'ight, it's time for me to go," he stated, getting the feeling that no matter what they discussed it would always end up about him and what he was doing.

"Kamari," she called out, stopping him as he turned to leave, "you can go now because you have that freedom, but if you don't make the right choices, you won't always have that luxury," she said, her voice as firm as her words.

Yet, her words fell on deaf ears as he turned and left.

CHAPTER 46

"God... aren't you tired?" inquired Sandy, while staring up into the sweat-drenched face of Mink, who she laid beneath as he vigorously pumped between her legs at a pace he'd been maintaining for well over an hour. "Mink," she continued, pushing on his chest with both hands when he didn't answer. "Mink, what's wrong with you? You haven't come yet," she added, pushing him until he rolled off her and sat up on the edge of the bed. "What's wrong with you?" she repeated, sitting up, her big breasts exposed and bouncing as she did so.

She stared at him as he sat with his back to her putting on his boxers.

"Nothing," he answered, snatching up his pants from the floor and going into the bathroom of their hotel room, closing the door behind him.

Staring at his reflection in the mirror, he did not like what he saw staring back at him, which to him, meant his high was wearing off. However, in truth, nothing was wrong with his appearance that anyone who knew him would notice as being out of the ordinary. If it were not for the fact that he had been going at it like a madman with Sandy without coming, she wouldn't have questioned him about his state of being. This, however, did not play into his line of thinking. The paranoia brought on by the cocaine had him believing he looked different in a way that could only be resolved with more cocaine.

Digging through the pockets of his jeans, which he held in his hand, he pulled out a vial of cocaine. Removing the cap, he sprinkled out two lines onto the sink and snorted each one into a nostril, all while holding onto his jeans. Placing the now half-empty vial of cocaine back into his pocket, he put on his jeans and glanced again at his reflection in the mirror

"Yeah, that's better," he said aloud to himself, smiling approvingly at what he saw.

"Mink, who are you talking to? I have to use the bathroom, too, you know," yelled Sandy from outside the door.

After throwing water on his face, he opened the door, which Sandy stood outside of naked, holding her clothes in her arm.

"It's all yours," he said, passing her as she stared at him not knowing what to make of his behavior. "Hurry up so we can get out of here," he added, as she moved past him into the bathroom.

"You have some nerve," she remarked, slamming the bathroom door.

CHAPTER 47

Coming to a stop in front of Sandy's house, Mink shut off the windshield wipers and cut off the engine. It had begun to rain as they left the hotel and headed out to a Caribbean restaurant on Boston Road in the Bronx where Sandy wanted to go for some curry chicken and rice. Sitting beside him with the bag containing just that in her lap, she waited for him to say something, as the sound of rain beating down upon the car filled the silence between them.

"Call me later," she said, giving up the wait.

"Yeah, a'ight," he answered more out of reaction than intention. "Tell your brother I said to come here. I need to talk to him," he added.

"Okay," she said, getting out the car and making a dash to the house in an effort not to get wet.

Five minutes passed before Dave came out with a purple hoody over his head, wearing jeans and a pair of New Balance. Jogging out to the car, he opened the door and slid into the passenger seat.

"What's going on with you, nigga? You ducking me or what?"

"It ain't nothing like that. I'm just..." he stammered, trying to get up the nerve to say what he needed to say.

"Just what, nigga?" broke in Mink, staring across at him, as Dave looked straight ahead unable to look him in the face.

"Just trying to figure out some things in my head."

"Don't they got doctors for that shit?" Mink replied in an effort to bring a little humor into the situation and avoid where Dave was going with it.

"Yo, seriously, man. Shit hasn't been the same since that shit went down with Staggs."

"Yeah, shit ain't ever gonna be the same without him; that was our nigga. I know. I feel you. He's gonna be missed forever."

"No, it's not just that. It's more to it than that," he said, raising his voice, determined to free himself of the burden he had been carrying since Staggs' death. Turning to face Mink for the first time since entering the car, he went on. "It's this life, man, the shit we been doing. It's not right."

Mink didn't answer; he just stared across at him like he was a stranger.

195

"It didn't have to happen like that to Staggs," he went on, forcing Mink to look away. "There's nothing left of him but memories, and no matter how hard I try to think about the good ones, they all end the same way, with him lying dead, a bullet hole in his head. Everything we did never seemed real to me until that night," he said, watching Mink, who reached into the pocket of his jeans, pulled out the vial of cocaine, placed it to his nose, and snorted the remainder of the cocaine.

"Yo, what are you doing?" Dave asked.

"What does it look like I'm doing?" Mink replied, without looking at him.

"Cocaine?" he said, as Mink cracked the window and tossed out the empty vial. "You're doing coke, Mink? See, that's proof that this shit is getting to you, too."

"Nah, this is proof that I'm not like you," he said, turning angrily on him. "That Staggs was nothing like you. You see, for us it's always been real. But, for you, it was just some Catholic schoolboy's little game. Now get the fuck outta my car before I forget I ever knew you," he said, starting the engine as he turned away from him.

Dazed by Mink's words, Dave slowly exited the car and briefly held the door open as he glanced inside at Mink

196

before closing it. He stood in front of his house watching as Mink drove down the block out of sight, the rain running down his face, concealing the tears that fell from his eyes brought on by the truth of Mink's words.

CHAPTER 48

The black Lincoln Town Car with tinted windows was parked in front of Sylvia's Soul Food Restaurant on 125th and Lenox Avenue. In the front seat, Faison sat, along with the driver, a tall dark-skinned man of Nigerian descent, who drove exclusively for him. In the backseat is where Kamari sat.

They had just returned from Grant projects, where Faison introduced Kamari to a kid named Travis, who had recently come home from prison. Before going to prison, he supposedly had most of Grant projects on lock. Kamari met with him to decide whether to sanction a deal, in which Faison would give him a half a key on consignment so he could get back on his feet. In return, he would bring all his future business to them, which could be anywhere from two to five keys a week once he regained his hold on the projects. To Kamari, the gains outweighed the risks. Therefore, he agreed to do the deal, which would be handled by Faison, being that he vouched for Travis.

Now as they sat parked in front of Sylvia's, the place of their second and final meeting for the day, Kamari checked his watch.

"Yo, what's up? It's twenty after three. Where's your man at?" Kamari asked.

"He'll be here," answered Faison, scanning the area for his man, the dust dealer who wanted to get into the coke game.

"He picked the spot and time, so the least he could do is be on time."

"Here he comes," said Faison, as a pine green Pathfinder pulled up and parked in front of them.

The driver side door opened and out stepped a heavyset dude, who stood about 6'1" with a caramel brown complexion, sporting a Cesar, and wearing black sweats, a green and white polo shirt, and a pair of green and white Nike Air. Kamari watched him close the door and move toward them, thinking to himself that the kid, who had to weigh close to 300 pounds, moved well for his size. Reaching the Lincoln, he got in back with Kamari, rocking the car as he flopped down next to him. As if on cue, the driver got out at the same time and went into Sylvia's to place an order for Faison.

"Damn, bee, you're looking good," exclaimed Faison, smiling as he turned in his seat to face the kid.

"I can't complain. It's good living," he replied in a smooth voice caught between high and low, which sounded to Kamari like he was the type never to raise his voice.

199

"This right here is my man Big Hamp," said Faison, still smiling as he introduced him to Kamari.

"Hamp, this is my man I've been telling you about, Kamari."

"Yeah, what's happening, money?" he said as they shook hands. "Faison told me how you're plugged in to those peoples, and right now, I'm in the process of looking for a good connect. I'm willing to take a couple at whatever price they're asking to start out. But, after that, they're going to have to come down, and I'll go up on how many I cop," he said, wasting no time as he stared across at Kamari, who didn't like none of what he was hearing.

"How much did Faison tell you they were asking?" asked Kamari, trying to see if things were as they sounded.

"What? Sixteen, right?" he answered, looking from Faison back to Kamari. "At that price, I'll take two or three, but like I said, after that, they're going to have to work with me."

"A'ight, I'ma see what I can do, and we'll get back to you," Kamari said, not needing or wanting to hear anymore.

"Yeah, yeah, bee, give us a few days," chimed in Faison, as Big Hamp opened the door to get out.

"You know how to reach me," he said, shaking Faison's hand and then Kamari's, before exiting the car and heading back to his truck.

"So what do you think?" asked Faison, while looking back at Kamari, who sat staring out the window in the direction of Sylvia's.

"I don't know. What do you think?" he asked, turning to face him.

"He's good peoples, a major nigga 'round Harlem, and…"

"So, for that, I should plug him into my connect?" he said, cutting him off, his face conveying the feelings behind the words.

"No, bee…" Faison began as the driver returned with his order. "Hold on. Give us a minute," he said, taking the food.

"That's what it sounded like to me," Kamari said, as the driver closed the door.

"It's not always about turning a profit. Sometimes you do things to build ties that pay off later down the line. That's in any business."

"This ain't *any* business. In this business, later is as good as never, and besides, what's a nigga gonna do for me in a

201

business he's trying to get into? I need a heroin connect. Does he have one of those?" Kamari asked.

"I don't know, but I'll check. Meanwhile, just think about it, that's all," Faison replied, then turned around and motioned to the driver that they were ready to go.

"Yeah, I will," he replied, knowing he had already made up his mind.

Just then, his beeper went off. Picking up his cell phone, he dialed the number appearing on the screen.

"Yeah, what up? … Get the fuck outta here … When? … Yeah… I'm on my way," he said, disconnecting the call.

"Everything all right?" asked Faison.

"My man in New Rochelle got knocked. They raided his crib and locked him and his mother up," he answered, shaking his head. "Take me back out the way," he added, visibly upset as they pulled off.

CHAPTER 49

"Hold it," said Kamari, handing the framed portrait of a male lion lying in an open field in Africa with his mate and cubs to Erica. "I'll be right back," he declared, leaving her in his bedroom while he went to get something to hang the portrait that was a surprise gift from her, which she had only given to him minutes ago.

She had seen it while out shopping with her mother, and remembered him telling her how lions were his favorite animals because they were synonymous with strength and beauty. Therefore, she had to get it for him.

"What are you going to do with that?" she asked, smiling at him as he returned with a chair and a wooden meat tenderizer from the kitchen.

"I'ma show you," he exclaimed, the expression on his face serious like he was about to put in some real work.

"You need a hammer. That's not a hammer," she laughed.

"In the hood, this is a hammer, and if you had on a pair of hard bottom shoes, they would be considered a hammer, too," he explained, keeping her in laughter, while she stood holding the portrait and looking up at him as he hammered a nail into the wall with the meat tenderizer. "Get that," he said, hearing someone knocking on the door and figuring it to be Marco, whom he was expecting.

Setting the portrait against the wall, Erica went to answer the door. Bending down, he picked up the portrait and hung it on the wall as Erica called him to the door.

"Kamari," she called again from the hall, as he stepped down from the chair and examined his work before going to see who was at the door.

"Yeah, who is it?" he said, stepping out into the hall and stopping in mid stride.

At the end of the hall, Erica stood holding the door open, as Amiena stood in the doorway. Both were staring him down; both were beautiful in her own right. Ameina's face held a look of accusation opposed to Erica's, whose was one of confusion. Gathering his composure, he proceeded down the hall pass Erica to Ameina, taking her by the arm.

"What are you doing here?" he said under his breath, while trying to lead her away from the apartment and Erica.

"What?" she shouted. "I thought you said you don't fuck with her no more and you couldn't stand being around her. Now here she is at your apartment," she protested.

"Stop fucking lying. You don't even know her," he responded in a voice loud enough for Erica to hear, as he glanced down the hall at her and saw tears forming in her eyes before she disappeared into the apartment. "Come on," he said, taking a firm grip on Ameina's arm, pulling her down the hall to the elevator and hitting the button several times.

"No, you're a fucking liar, Kamari. You talked all that shit about her, and here you are with her," she yelled in the direction of his apartment, hoping her words carried to the girl whom she had no idea as to her identity. However, having seen her, she knew she was beautiful enough to be a threat.

"Stop yelling before you get me kicked out of my apartment," he said tight jawed, as the elevator arrived and he dragged her onto it. "What's wrong with you?" he asked, staring at her as he pressed the button for the lobby.

"There ain't nothing wrong with me, but something gotta be wrong with me to come and see you."

"Without calling, yeah," he yelled.

"Motherfucker, I don't say that shit to you when you pop up at my house."

"Yo, watch your fucking mouth. What was all that extra shit? You don't even know her."

"I know she was in your apartment, and that's enough," she responded, twisting up her mouth as the doors to the elevator opened on the lobby.

Leading her out of the building, he walked her over to where she had parked her girlfriend's Benz, which she had borrowed to come and see him.

"Go home," he said, letting her go as they came to a stop.

"I ain't going nowhere and leaving you alone with that bitch. You must be crazy," she said with the attitude he had grown fond of, but at the moment, it was making his blood boil.

"Yo, why are you calling her a bitch when you're the one acting like a bitch?"

"Oh, you taking up for her?"

"Yo, we're not even fucking with each other like that," he said heatedly.

"Yeah, well, all that's going to change, because you don't be coming to my house and finding no niggas answering the door. I'm not going for it. You don't need all those other bitches no more. Anything you want and need, I can give you," she said, and he could not help but laugh. "It's not funny," she exclaimed, laughing herself as Erica came out the building and got into her car.

Kamari didn't notice her leaving until he heard her pulling off.

"Fuck," he mumbled, as he watched her speed off. "Shit, my keys," he said, realizing he was locked out of his apartment as Marco pulled up in a gray Mazda RX7. "Give me a minute," he yelled out to him, holding up a hand. "Look, she's gone, and I'm locked out. Now, can you go home and I'll call you later."

"Al right, but you better call me, because we need to talk."

"I ain't better do nothing. Who the fuck do you think you talking to?" he said angrily, gazing at her.

"Can you please call me so we can talk?" she said, with a pleading expression on her face.

"Yeah, a'ight, that's more like it," he said, while she smiled at him and ducked into her girlfriend's car.

As she pulled off, Kamari walked over to where Marco waited and slid into the passenger seat.

"What's the matter with you?" asked Marco, looking over at him.

"Take me to my aunt Stacey's to get the extra set of keys to my apartment, and I'll explain it to you on the way," he said, as Marco shifted the sports car into first gear and peeled off.

CHAPTER 50

After picking up the keys from his aunt's, Kamari ran a few errands with Marco, who teased him about his dilemma with the females. When they parted, he went about his business of collecting money, making sure his people had what they needed to supply the demand of the streets. He then met with Grant, who he bailed out along with his mother. The lawyer he hired to handle the case, who was his personal attorney, got Grant a plea agreement to probation since it was his first arrest, which included the charges being dropped against his mother. Having made up his mind that there was no need to open back up in New Rochelle with all the other things he had going on, he told Grant to lay low for awhile until the heat was off him, which he knew would be a long time. Throughout all of these events, he remained preoccupied with what had transpired earlier with Erica and what he would say to her. The answer of which still eluded him as he pulled up in front of her house.

Hopping out his jeep, he walked over to the front door and rang the bell. When several minutes passed without an answer, he rang it again. The light came on in the foyer, and he could hear the locks being disengaged. The door opened, and Erica stood in faded jeans worn at the knees, a gray fleece Nike t-shirt, and a pair of slippers. Her damp hair hung freely down her back, and looked as if she just got out of the shower. The foyer light provided the necessary illumination with which to admire her flawless skin and stirring beauty, as she stood staring at him disapprovingly.

"Look, that girl…" he began, attempting to explain.

"Kamari, I don't want to hear it," she said, cutting him off as she crossed her arms in a no-nonsense manner, letting the door close on her back.

"Listen, just let me tell you…"

"Tell me what, Kamari?" she said, cutting him off again. "I asked did you have someone else. I'm not stupid. I figured as much and asked you…" she continued, trailing off as she fought back tears.

"I'm sorry," he apologized, reaching out for her.

"No, get off me," she cried, pushing him away. "All this time we've been together I thought you'd get the picture. That you would one day come around and see, but you don't get it," she said in tears, watching him as he watched her.

The tables having turned, it was now him who stood in confusion.

"Yeah, you don't get it, Kamari," she repeated in a whisper, taking off the bracelet he'd given her and tossing it to the ground in front of him as she disappeared inside the apartment and closed the door, leaving him at a loss for words.

She did not understanding that for him, the picture had been shattered, and that it would be a long time before he could put it back together, thanks to Natasha. Bending over, he picked up the bracelet and made his way back to his jeep. Glancing up at her apartment window, he pulled off. Nearing the corner, he was consumed with feelings of guilt as he struggled to understand what he felt for Erica, when out of nowhere, a late model four-door Bonneville sped out of a parking lot to his left, cutting him off.

"What the fuck," he cursed, slamming on the brakes, as the back and passenger side door swung open on the Bonneville and two hooded dudes emerged with guns in hand and began firing.

CHAPTER 51

Erica stood in the bathroom wiping away tears, as she looked in the mirror, upset with herself for crying in front of him when she told herself she wouldn't.

"Damn you, Kamari," she said angrily, as the sound of the gunfire echoed outside, startling her. "Oh, my God!"

She ran from the bathroom to the front of the apartment, knowing it was Kamari.

CHAPTER 52

Kamari threw himself down across the front seat as the bullets shattered the windshield, spraying him with glass as they passed above him, ripping through the seats and blowing out the rear window. Frantically, he grabbed the base of the steering wheel with his left hand and threw the jeep into reverse with the other, while stepping on the gas. Tires spinning, the jeep jolted backwards, colliding up against parked cars as he struggled to keep it straight, praying that no cars were coming down the block. While moving backwards away from the gunfire, he glanced up in the rearview mirror. The incident with Erica was now forgotten, as his every movement and thought was being dictated by his basic instinct to survive.

Meanwhile, a terrified Erica watched from her living room window as he sped backwards past her house followed by his pursuers.

CHAPTER 53

Inside the emergency room of Mount Vernon Hospital, Erica stood where she'd been waiting for over an hour in the same attire she had on earlier, her arms crossed, car keys dangling in one hand and Kamari's cell phone in the other, as she spoke nervously to two uniformed officers questioning her about what she'd seen. The emergency room doors burst open, drawing her attention, and in walked Mink, followed by Knox and Blass.

Though she and Mink had never met other than the phone call she had made that brought him to the hospital, they recognized each other immediately. She knew him as somebody Kamari would bond with just by the way he entered the room, his presence dominating and commanding, and he viewed her as the type of female with all the qualities that drew his friend like an art collector to fine art. Ignoring the two officers as if they didn't exist, which to him they didn't, Mink walked directly up to her.

"You Erica, the one who called me?" he asked, as she nodded and moved a strand of loose hair from her face.

"Excuse me, may I ask your relation to the victim?" said one of the officers.

214

Turning to face him with a look of disgust on his face, Mink started to say something that might have earned him a night in jail, just as Kamari emerged from the operating area, a bandage on his forehead and several small cuts on his face caused by the shattering glass.

Erica immediately ran up to him, throwing herself into his arms, her earlier encounter with Ameina at his apartment forgotten.

"You ready to be outta here?" asked Mink under the watchful eyes of the two officers, as two plainclothes detectives that had been interrogating Kamari in back for an hour stepped out into the lobby staring curiously at them.

"Yeah," he answered, taking Erica's hand and leading the way outside, where he told Mink and them to follow him to his place before getting in Erica's car with her.

"Did I do the right thing?" she asked, starting the car and looking over at him.

"Yeah, you did a'ight," he answered, smiling wearily, his brush with death taking its toll on him both mentally and physically. "No, you did better than that. You did good," he added, extracting a smile from her as they pulled off.

She had called the police, and hearing the approaching sirens, his pursuers gave up the chase and fled, leaving him to be the one the police apprehended until Erica arrived on the scene to explain the situation. Afterwards, the police took him to the hospital for treatment, where they continued to treat him like a prisoner. He had rather taken his chances with the gunmen. At least with them he knew what he was dealing with, unlike the police who were at times bad guys pretending to be good guys. Nevertheless, he couldn't tell her that. So, yeah, she did good.

CHAPTER 54

Outside his apartment building, he spoke briefly with Mink and the others about what happened before they left him to get some rest, with plans to return in the morning. Once inside his apartment, he showered, while Erica phoned her mother. Getting out the shower, he went into the bedroom, where she sat on the bed arguing with her mother over the phone.

"It's not like that, Ma," she said, raising her voice as Kamari slipped into a pair of sweats and laid down on the bed behind her. "Yes, I know…no, he's not…I just know… you can't say that because you don't know…they don't know, and he doesn't even know," she continued as he listened, running his fingers through her hair, knowing he was the topic of their conversation. "Yes, no… all right, tomorrow… yes, bye, Ma," she said, hanging up and turning around to lay down in his arms, as she rested her head on his bare chest.

"What did she say?" he asked.

"It doesn't matter."

"Tell me. I wanna know. What did she say?" he asked again, waiting for an answer.

"That being around you, I'm going to get myself killed," she finally answered.

"She might be right," he replied truthfully, while moving back strands of hair from her face as he stared down at her from where he laid elevated by pillows. "Erica, maybe…"

"Shhhh…" she said, stopping him in mid sentence. "Can we just lay here? I just want to be near you, that's all, please," she whispered, her words trailing off as she listened to the sound of his heartbeat, thanking God he was alive.

"Sure," he replied, as he glanced up at the portrait of the lions whose eyes seemed to be staring back at him judgingly, giving him an uneasy feeling that passed quickly.

He was not sure if it was real or his imagination, but in the end, he found a place for it with the rest of the day's craziness, as he closed his eyes and drifted off to sleep with Erica in his arms.

CHAPTER 55

In deep thought, Kamari sat in the back of the Lincoln Town Car with Knox to his left, while Faison rode up front with his driver, as they headed out to Grant projects to meet with Travis. The streets were quiet on who was behind the attempt on his life, which had him a little paranoid whenever he moved. He even let Mink and them talk him into wearing a bulletproof vest until they found out who was responsible.

He fell back from Erica, taking into consideration her mother's concerns, and only spoke to her over the phone. Their conversations often led to questions about the other female and what was it that she had that her, Erica, did not. These questions more often than not were answered with silence. What Erica wanted from him was a normal relationship, but he tried that with Natasha and it didn't work. On the other hand, what Ameina offered was anything but normal, and this agreed with him in the life he was living.

The big Lincoln turned off Broadway into the parking lot of Grant projects, and as instructed by Kamari, the driver drove pass Travis, who stood in the middle of the lot waiting. Continuing down to the end of the lot, the driver made a U-turn as Kamari surveyed the area. Coming to a stop behind several parked cars next to Travis, Knox got out and motioned for him to take his place, while the driver vacated his position to Knox and waited outside up against the front end of the car.

"What's going on, bee," asked Faison, looking back at Travis, who was about his age, in his early 30's, and stood 5' 11", with dark complexion and sporting low, wavy hair with a goatee.

Travis was simply dressed in jeans, T-shirt, and a pair of white Reebok classics, and was all business as he exchanged greetings with everyone.

"Psss," he breathed, shaking his head and indicating that things weren't going good. "Remember how I told y'all that I held most of the projects before I fell," he went on, not expecting a reply.

"Well, my plan was to start back with two buildings and move on from there. Things were going smooth up until the other night. The young boys that took over when I fell didn't say nothing the first couple of days we set up shop. I guess they figured because they had the area for a while their clientele would speak for itself. But the coke you gave us is some top-notch shit, and when their regulars started passing them up for us, the shit hit the fan."

"Hit the fan how?" Kamari asked, watching him intently.

"They moved on my peoples in both buildings, one of which I grew up in and that I'm staying in right now. One of my mans got hit, and we put it in on two of their peoples."

"Any lives lost?" Kamari continued, already forming a plan in his head.

"No, no bodies."

"How about product?"

"No losses there, but I'm sitting on what I've got left until this shit is settled. My team is not that deep right now, and I don't want to take any chances."

"You want me to bring some BK niggas in to back him up," Knox asked.

"Nah, if we do that, it'll be too hot for anyone to get any money," answered Faison.

"Yeah, that's the last result. That's if it's worth the trouble," said Kamari. "Are these dudes all with the same crew?"

"The same run by a kid named Chauncy out of the 23rd Street side of the projects."

"What kind a nigga is he?" asked Faison.

"I can't really say. I don't know him. But from what I've seen of him, he looks like the typical young cat, all show," answered Travis, twisting up his face.

"You got someone you can send to talk to him?" Kamari asked.

"Talk to him for what?" Travis spit, frowning.

"For a sit- down," said Faison, understanding Kamari's line of questioning.

"Between you, him, and us...somewhere public... a restaurant for lunch or something. Tell him he's welcome to bring two of his people," Kamari proposed.

"Yeah, I'll see what I can do, but you can't talk to these young boys. They only respect one thing, and that's the barrel of a gun. But, like I said, I'll see what I can do. Here's five on what I owe," Travis said, handing Kamari a knot of bills. "Give me a couple of days," he added.

"Just make it happen, bee," said Faison.

"I'll do what I can," he replied, exiting the car as Knox came around and returned to the back seat.

"I like the way you think," Faison said, smiling at Kamari as they pulled out of the lot.

222

CHAPTER 56

Mink arrived home after being out all night to find his sister and Shonda, who was now seven months pregnant with his child, seated at the kitchen table staring at him as he entered. Closing the door behind him, he ignored them and headed for his room. Inside his room, he removed a .357 from the waistband of his pants, as Shonda came and stood in the doorway watching.

"Mink, you can't still be mad at me for wanting to have our child," she said, her tone filled with the ridiculousness of his actions.

Continuing to ignore her, he placed the gun on top of his dresser and proceeded to empty his pockets.

"Am I wrong for loving you so much that I want to have your child? Am I? Huh?" she tried reasoning, watching him remove his jewelry and take off his shirt. "Am I wrong for being afraid I might lose you to the streets and be left with nothing but what if's?" she went on, raising her voice at him as he took a seat on the bed and began removing his pants. "Mink, why are you acting like this?" she cried, tears falling from her eyes as he got up and walked toward her in his boxers.

His eyes were cast down, refusing to acknowledge her, numb and exhausted from the cocaine he had been sniffing that kept him out all night. She was emotionally exhausted, as the tears ran steadily down her face from the pain of being treated as if she did not exist by the man she loved and whose child she carried. Mink got within inches of her and stopped. Then he reached out as if he were going to touch her, console her even, but instead turned off the light switch to the right of the door where she stood. Stunned and shaken by his actions, she watched in the darkness as his shadowy figure climbed into bed, before turning and running from the house in tears.

CHAPTER 57

Ramos was an Italian restaurant located where Harlem meets downtown Manhattan, situated on the side of Manhattan between One Police Plaza and the South Seaport. Faison chose it as the place for the sit-down because if either side did not trust the other, they could at least rest assure that no one would be stupid enough to try anything right up under the police's nose. Kamari sat at a corner table in the back of the restaurant, a location he always looked for whenever dining out, preferring the ambience of obscurity over visibility. With him sat Faison and Travis, waiting on the arrival of Chauncy and his people for what would appear to be a late lunch amongst friends.

"Excuse me, are you gentlemen ready to order?" asked the waitress, a slim brunette with huge breasts that had Travis mesmerized as she stood between him and Faison, pen and pad in hand.

"Can we just get something to drink for now? We're waiting on friends," replied Faison.

"Sure, no problem. What would you like?"

"Let's get a bottle of white Zinfandel."

"Yeah, that sounds good," said Travis, while openly staring at her breast.

"An ice tea with lemon for me, please," said Kamari, laughing at Travis.

"Okay then, I'll be back shortly," replied the waitress, departing.

"Hey yo, bee, you ain't get that jail shit out your system yet? Staring at that woman like you still locked up. You free, bee, so act like it," said Faison, making them all laugh.

"Is that them?" asked Kamari, nodding toward a baldheaded, dark- skinned kid entering the restaurant followed by two others, one of whom was tall and light complexioned, and the second who was dark and beefy, and looked like he could be the baldheaded kid's brother.

The baldheaded kid stood about 5'10", and was dressed in an Atlanta Braves jersey, jeans, and a pair of white and gray Nike Cortez. He couldn't have been older than nineteen, and his two companions not much older than that.

"Yeah, that's him and his brother, Cabbage," answered Travis. "And the tall, light skin kid is his lieutenant, Bullet," he added.

"Please, have a seat," Faison said, with a gesture of his hand. "My name is Faison. I'm glad y'all agreed to sit down with us and discuss this thing like men," he continued, as they took a seat across from him, Kamari, and Travis.

To this, Chauncy responded with a nod. As he stared across at Faison, trying to read him, the waitress returned with their drinks, taking the orders of their new arrivals before departing.

"Me and Travis go back a long ways, and upon his release from prison, we entered into an agreement. That's why I'm here, on behalf of that agreement. Now, I'm pretty sure we're all in the game for the same reason, which is the money, and if it's a war over the projects, nobody will make any money. So why don't we try to come to some kind of agreement that will avoid a war?" Faison suggested.

"Look, money, what you said makes a lot of sense," Chauncy began, pausing as the waitress returned and sat the drinks on the table before leaving. "So you should have no problem understanding where I'm coming from. Travis was the man back in the day when he basically ran the projects, but that was then. Those days are over."

"What you mean those days are over?" interrupted Travis, getting upset.

"Yo, bee, let him have his say," said Faison, while staring angrily over at Travis, who was seated to his left. "You're going to get your chance. Go ahead, bee. I'm sorry about that."

"Like I was saying," he continued, picking up where he left off without once looking over at Travis, even though he had interrupted him.

Kamari observantly took all of this in, his respect growing by the minute for the kid who Travis had pegged as a typical, all-show young boy.

"He fell and we rose," Chauncy went on. "Now he comes back and expects us to hand it all back over to him. Well, the game's not played like that," he said slowly for emphasis, his point sharp and to the heart as he glanced over for the first time at Travis, who sat steaming.

"You're right," interjected Kamari, drawing glances of disapproval from Faison and Travis.

"Yeah, and who are you?" asked Chauncy, gazing over at him, a question that had been on his mind since he sat down.

"That's my…" began Faison, as Kamari held up a hand, cutting him off.

"I'm you," Kamari answered smiling.

228

"You're me?" replied Chauncy with a laugh, as he glanced from his brother to his lieutenant, who shared in his laughter.

"Yeah, I'm you," repeated Kamari. "I'm you in that like you, I'm a young dude in a game that for years, all its major players have been older dudes, but crack has changed all that. Now I'm a major player, you're a major player, and just because we're young shouldn't mean the rules don't apply. So let's play by the rules; me and you."

"Ain't this a bitch? You are me," Chauncy said, grinning over at him, as his brother and lieutenant began smiling approvingly, followed by smiles from Faison and Travis.

However, unlike the rest of them, whose smiles were genuine, theirs were not. Theirs were smiles of necessity because they represented the older dudes.

When they finished eating, an agreement was reached between them. Kamari would supply Chauncy with a better product at a cheaper price than he was now paying. In return, he would give Travis the buildings on 125th, maintaining those from 23rd and over. It was a compromise to avoid unnecessary violence; one that Kamari walked away from feeling good about, but not everyone shared those same feelings.

229

CHAPTER 58

Out front, crowds ranging in sizes and genders stood around conversing or just taking in the sights of Harlem's nightlife at its peak. There were tour buses filled with many different ethnicities, who came from all over to witness and be a part of Harlem's oldest and most popular cultural event, Amateur Night at the Apollo Theater. As always, since its conception, its most dominating presence remained those of the streets' underworld, from the time of pimps and players, dope dealers and number runners, to at one point even being rumored to be owned by one of Harlem's most notorious dealers. Now it was the crack dealers, with their expensive cars, lining the streets with New York, New Jersey, and Philadelphia tags, who were most prevalent. They were young, flamboyant, and brazen in life. They were the ghettos newest role models and trendsetters. As they went, so went the streets.

Double- parking across from the Apollo, Kamari stepped out of a pearl black 626 Mazda Coupe wearing a black Nike velour sweat suit and a pair of black suede and cranberry Nike Cortez. With him were Knox and Stan, who have been convincing him of late to get out more and enjoy himself. For him, waking up each morning to face the day with the knowledge that there were those who wanted him dead, and having no idea as to whom they were, was no way to live. He was strongly considering going out to DC and setting up something until they could find out who was behind the guns aimed at him. Meanwhile, he had decided that whatever was going to happen would happen, so he might as well enjoy himself.

Crossing the street, they stood near the entrance of the Apollo as people filtered out. Stan spotted some Harlem females he knew amongst the crowd and called them over to him. Kamari, who stood off to the right of him with Knox, was busy watching a group of females grab up a rapper from Brooklyn, who had a hit album out, to take pictures with them, when the sound of females screaming drew his attention. Turning to his right, he watched as a crowd of mostly females moved toward a black Bentley pulling up in front of the Apollo.

"What the fuck is wrong with them?" Kamari asked, as the mob formed around the Bentley, not giving whoever was inside a chance to get out.

"It's the heavyweight champ of the world," replied one of the females Stan was talking with.

"Yo, Kamari, Ameina likes red BM's," remarked Knox, tapping him and nodding toward Ameina, who stood talking to a dude in a red BM that sat double-parked on the side of the street where they stood.

Kamari knew the dude in the BM to be a member of a well-known R&B group out of Harlem. He had also seen him a few times in the Vernon hanging out with Big Joop and DJ Classy.

"Yeah, I see her. Now ask me do I care," he said, as she glanced over in his direction, pleased with the fact that he'd seen her.

They weren't speaking, which wasn't anything unusual between the two of them. They stayed going at it about one thing or another, separating for a week or two and ending up back together. Therefore, what she was doing now wasn't anything new. Once, she even had a dude in a Benz drive her up to Mount Vernon, so they could pass by where Kamari stood with his people. Knox, who was present at the time, wanted to snatch the dude out the Benz and pistol whip him. Kamari just laughed, jumped in his ride, and headed out to Queens. Before he reached his destination, she beeped him from home, explaining how she made the dude take her home. It was like after the thing with Erica, she felt the need to let him know there were dudes who wanted her, and that he should be honored she was with him.

"Yo, y'all wanna shoot over to the Palladium when we leave here?" asked Stan, turning away from the females to pose the question to Kamari and Knox.

"I don't care. Whatever y'all wanna do," answered Kamari, watching as Chauncy and his brother got out of a white Acura legend and proceeded across the street toward him.

At the same time, Ameina strutted away from the BM in jeans that clung to her like a second skin and back over to her friends, drawing stares from them as she passed, which made Kamari laugh.

"Damn, you see the ass on that one?" remarked Chauncy, as him and his brother reached Kamari and Knox.

"What's up?" Kamari said, smiling and giving them five. "Yo, these my people right here," he added, introducing everybody.

"So what's going on? I didn't know this was your scene. I'm a regular out here, and I never seen you out here," said Chauncy jokingly.

"Yeah, you right. This ain't me, but what the fuck. A nigga gotta get out sometime."

"Yeah, I hear that shit. But, next time, let me know something and I'll get you some good seats."

"You doing it like that around here?" Kamari replied, acting as if he was in awe.

"What ! Yo, come on now. I'm a young Harlem knight. I got peoples, mannn…" he dragged on, making them all laugh.

They hung out in front of the Apollo for a while longer, with Chauncy introducing them to some of his people before leaving for the Palladium. During this time, Kamari witnessed Ameina and her friends talking to some dudes from Philly. At all this, Knox looked on in disapproval. He didn't like her, which he had expressed to Kamari. Kamari had responded by saying it wasn't for him to like her, but he had to respect her because Kamari liked her.

On their way to the Palladium, Knox sat in the back rolling a blunt, while Stan drove and Kamari sat back listening to Johnny Kemps "Just Got Paid". Kamari was feeling so relaxed that he removed his vest, which he complained was too hot and uncomfortable. He even let them talk him into smoking with them, something Oscar had never been able to accomplish.

When they reached the Palladium, the females Stan had been talking to at the Apollo were there. Inside, the place was packed with females of all shapes, colors, and races. Kamari ordered a few Heinekens, smoked a little more, danced, and enjoyed himself, completely forgetting about the business of the street for the first time since he'd gotten involved in dealing drugs. Never mind the fact that only weeks ago someone had tried to kill him. Who and why was as big a mystery as the Bermuda triangle was to the world, but for the moment, that, too, had been forgotten.

CHAPTER 59

"Why you wanna go out there?" Asked Blass in response to the news from Kamari that he was going to D.C.

"Why! Why not? We can't stay in one place forever. We need to branch out, explore new avenues, and there's no better time than now," he explained thinking of the unknown individuals who tried to kill him. "I'm going to set up shop myself. That's why I'm telling yall to see who wants to come with me and whose wants to stay here," he continued looking from him to Joel and Tubah who stood with him and Knocs in the parking-lot of the Metro-North train station in Mount Vernon.

"Who you going out there with Chew," said Blass the most vocal of the three.

aZZ"Nah, I'm doing my own thing, but I'mma touch base with him once I get out there."

"Who else you know out there?"

"Knocs man from around his way in Brooklyn was out there hustling with a crew. The dude that ran the crew was jerking everybody so they bounced on him. He knows the area and how shit works; for me that's enough. I can take it from there once I get there."

"How you know you can trust him?" Asked Tubah speaking for the first time.

"I'm not even gonna answer that," Kamari said not wanting to offend anyone. "Look all I need is one of yall to come with me to D.C. The rest will remain and keep things in order here. So what's up?"

"I ain't never hustle nowhere but here. I wouldn't feel right no place else, I'm staying here," answered Blass apologetically.

"That's cool my nigga I figured as much."

"Me too, I'm staying home," Tubah quickly added.

"Cool. What about you Joel?" Kamari asked forced to put him on the spot with Less turned addict.

"Fuck it I'll go," he answered feeling he had no choice.

"A'ight, that's what's up. I'll hit you and let you know when we're leaving," he said giving them all dap before turning and heading to his ride with Knox.

"I was getting ready to say, what kind of niggas you been fucking with," grinned Knox as they climbed into the car.

"Some people are afraid of change, but one out of three ain't bad. It gets me on base," he smiled beeping his horn at the rest of them as they all exited the parking-lot in their cars and went their separate ways.

CHAPTER 60

It was late in the evening as Kamari drove thinking about his meeting with Mink whose home he'd just left. As of late Mink hadn't been acting himself, and it wasn't one particular thing that Kamari could put his finger on, but when you've known someone as long as he'd known Mink you just know. He even addressed his concerns after filling him in on his plans for D.C. to which Mink responded by fixing him with a piercing smirk that was vintage Mink. Kamari laughed and brushed off his concerns, but now they were returning as he pulled to a stop at a light on the corner of 3rd and 1st Avenue. His thoughts were interrupted by the sight his sister Dahlia coming up the block with Natasha. Rolling up alongside of them he blew the horn drawing their attention.

"Hey, what's up Bruv," shouted Dahlia excitedly coming up to the passenger-side window as it came down. Natasha who remained standing on the sidewalk smiling over at them was looking good he thought glancing at her. In a wrap around flower print skirt that hugged her hips, a cream blouse with matching sandals, and her hair evenly cut draping her face. Her beauty was more apparent than the day he'd first noticed it.

"What you doing out this late," he scolded turning his attention back to his sister.

239

"I'm with Natasha," she exclaimed frowning.

"That's right she's with me and you don't have to worry cause I'm taking her home right now," broke in Natasha with a smile as she walked up beside Dahlia and peered through the window.

"Where y'all coming from this late anyway?" He asked her feigning anger.

"A girlfriend of mine's house," she explained all the while beaming at him.

"It's kinda later for you to be out by yourself to. Get in I'll take y'all home," he said motioning with his hand for them to get in.

"It's good to know you still care," she stated smiling.

"That's my Bruv," laughed Dahlia opening the door and climbing in back as Natasha waited before getting in front.

"I'mma drop you off first Dahlia," he said pulling off.

"Why can't I go with you to drop Natasha home?"

"Cause we're closer to Mommy's and you was going home anyway so that's where I'm taking you," he answered to which she responded by sucking her teeth and falling back in

240

the seat as Natasha glanced over at him. Within minutes they reached his mother's home where from the car he and Natasha watched as Dahlia made her way safely inside.

Placing the car in drive Kamari said, "You don't have to go home if you don't want to, you know."

"Where else am I going to go," she answered turning toward him.

"Home with me," he answered with a half smile pulling out into the street.

"Are you inviting me to stay the night with you?" She asked, her eyes on him as he drove.

"Yeah, I'm inviting you," he said coming to an erupt stop in the middle of a one way street and facing her.

"Then I accept," she said in a matter of fact kind of way that was absent of what she was really accepting.

CHAPTER 61

On the drive to Kamari's apartment Natasha noticed they'd passed several places twice, going in circles, and that he constantly glanced in the rear-view mirror. Aware of the life he lived she said nothing not wanting to know the reason behind his actions; even if he would tell her which she knew he would not.

Walking inside his apartment she was impressed but not surprised by how nicely furnished it was. She knew he had a unique taste for things. "I like this, it's you," she remarked surveying the place as he closed and locked the door behind them.

"Thanks. Come on," he said leading the way down a hall. "Right in here," he announced moving through an open door and switching on a light to reveal his bedroom.

Following him she came to stop in the middle of the room and watched as he moved over to a nightstand and removed a gun from the waistband of his pants and placed it on top the nightstand. "You changed," she said in an almost whisper.

"Everything changes, nothing stays the same," Kamari replied walking over to her and gazing into her eyes with slight amusement. To this she said nothing, only returning his gaze. Reaching out he begin undoing the buttons on her blouse as he leaned in bringing his lips to hers. She didn't know where they were going with this or where they would end up. If it would be the start of a new beginning or for just this one night, she didn't care. All that mattered was that he wanted her now and in that alone laid hope for the love she'd told him was meant forever.

CHAPTER 62

Hold up inside a room at the Comfort Inn located on H Street in the Chinatown section of Washington D.C. Kamari sat on one of the twin beds speaking to Tasheeva on the phone. Also in the room seated at a table drinking a vanilla Nutriment dressed in a black Raiders jacket, gray fleece shirt, black jeans, and his trademark black Reebok classics was Knox. "Ahh, shit," groaned Kamari rubbing his eyes as he hung up the phone and fell back on the bed.

"Tired?" Asked Knox fidgeting with the now empty Nutriment can.

"Yeah, staying up all night bagging that shit up then flying out here in the morning, why wouldn't I be."

"I'm good, that hour nap on the plane was good enough for me. So what's next?"

"First we gotta get this shit outta here. Then get some wheels and go check on Joel and Abe," he explained referring to Joel and Knox man Abe who was showing them the set up. "Plus I wanna try to catch up with Chew." "He in the same area we at?"

"Nah, he over here in north west on 14th and W."

"Yo, I ain't believe Abe but that shit worked just like he said," exclaimed Knox.

"Yeah I know, it was easy, almost to easy," replied Kamari with a smirk referring to how they'd set up shop in South East D.C. Arriving they'd put Joel and Abe up in a room at the Ramada on 15th and Rhode Island then went across town and got the room at the Comfort Inn. From there they returned in a cab picking them up and headed out to Melon in South East, the block Abe use to hustle on. A block he'd told Kamari was known for dropping bodies, but was a two to three key a week block. So armed with a sample of their product and guns they went talking to feigns on the block trying to find one who lived in the block and didn't already have dealers dealing out of their apartment. They weren't able to find one on Malone, but they were able to get one on the next block over, which was Newcomb.

Malone and Newcomb were connected by an alley that ran the length of both with walkways running along the sides of houses and buildings leading into it. This provided various escape routes from police as well as ambush sites for potential enemies and stickup kids. The apartment was resided in by a crack addicted husband and wife named Norm and Sophia. At an agreement of a hundred dollars a day which was the equivalent of two fifties. A piece of crack in a mini zip lock bag about the size of a nickel. They

245

allowed Kamari to deal out of their apartment. And to establish a clientele he offered an additional fifty to them or any of their get high buddies for every ten customers they brought over from Malone to cop. All this had taken place within hours of arriving in D.C. Now they sat waiting on Tasheeva to get the remainder of the coke they'd brought out of the hotel.

"What's up, why you say it like that," asked Knox raising his eyebrows.

"Nah, aint no reason. It was just easy that's all," he answered as the phone rung. "Yeah,......Yeah, that's good," he replied into the receiver grinning as someone knocked on the door. He watched as Knox got up to open it. "A'ight, we'll be there in a few," he said placing the phone down as Tasheeva entered the room.

"Ayyy, Boo," she smiled walking over hugging and kissing him on the cheek as he rose from the bed to greet her. She'd decided to go back to school after Monique got married and had her baby.

"Damn girl," he exclaimed overwhelmed by her reaction to as Knocs sat back at the table grinning at him.

"Look at you, it's been too long," she said stepping back looking him over appraisingly.

"Nah, look at you. Your looking good as always," he threw back and she responded by spinning around and coming to a stop facing him with her hands on her hips for his approval. And his approval she had in her conservative fitting wheat colored linen pants suit, her hair immaculately done as always with black lacquer looking curls spiraling down the sides of her face, a pair of designer shades setting on top her head, and open toe black four inch platforms adding to her height. She was a picture of class and beauty.

"Yo, cut it out will you," he joked and she bust out into her cute southern tainted laughter. "This right here Tasheeva is my man Knox."

"Hi," she smiled extending her hand.

"Nice to meet you," replied Knox standing to shake her hands as Kamari reached under the bed pulling out a blue overnight bag.

"Same here," she said with a smile before turning back to Kamari as he was removing a black plastic bag from the overnight bag. "Where's the other guy you ran with, the dark skinned one from that night at the club in New York?"

"He's back in New York. He's good though," he answered and she just nodded. "Here take this," he said handing her the plastic bag of coke which she placed inside a black Coach bag she carried. "Let's get outta here," he continued retrieving the hotel key from the nightstand beside the phone. "O'yeah, I almost forgot. That was Joel on the phone. They ran out of work an hour and a half after we left," he grinned leading the way to the door.

CHAPTER 63

Driving Tasheeva's sky blue 88 Honda Accord Kamari turned onto Newcomb from Martin Luther King Jr. Boulevard in South East and pulled to a stop in front of the house they were dealing out of. Jumping out the passenger seat Knox trotted inside with the package while Kamari found a place to park. At the door of the apartment located on the first floor toward the back of the hall Knox stood after knocking. Abe opened the door with a nine millimeter in hand. "Yo, dem been comin like mad," he exclaimed in his Jamaican accent closing the door as Knox stepped inside what was the living room of the small one bedroom apartment.

"That's why we came straight here," said Knox pulling a bag containing five thousand in product from the crotch of his pants and tossing it to Joel who sat on a couch counting money on a coffee table, a shotgun beside him.

"Where's Kamari?" asked Joel catching the bag.

"He's parking the car," he answered moving over to the couch and sitting down next to him as Abe remained standing by the door.

"Two hours after we left, huh," he remarked looking from Joel to Abe.

"I think it was faster than that," replied Joel.

"What me tell yah bout dis spot ere," exclaimed Abe smiling over at him.

"Me not gon lie, but at first me not believe but it like yah say," said Knox as someone knocked on the door. "That be Kamari, Star," he announced watching as Abe opened the door letting him in.

"What's up yall, is this the real thing or what," smiled Kamari holding his hands out as he stepped through the door.

"It's real," replied Joel motioning to the money in front of him. "Twenty-five hundred an hour the first day on the job."

"See what me tell yah, yah not see nuttin yet," added Abe standing next to Kamari making them all laugh.

"Well I brought another five. I wanna see it happen again and then we'll double it to ten at a time," he said as Norm entered the room from the adjoining kitchen.

"Hayyy… Boss Man, how yall liking the Nation's Capital so far?" He asked smiling up at Kamari with glazed over eyes.

"I'm enjoying myself. How about you, my people taking care of you and the wife?"

"I ain't got no complaints," he answered throwing his hands in the air, one of which held a crack-pipe.

"That's good," smiled Kamari as someone knocked on the door and Norm turned and went back to the kitchen.

"I got it," said Abe turning and doing just that after peering through the peephole. Holding the gun at his side he held the door open as a tall light skinned dude came in with a wad of money in his hand. He didn't look like a crack-head Kamari thought observing him as he came inside with Abe shutting the door behind him.

"What's up money," said Kamari watching him closely.

"Hold, I want yall to know I got my piece on me," he announced raising his shirt revealing the handle of a gun tucked in the waistband of his jeans.

"A'ight, it's not a problem this time. Just take it out and set it down," he said since Abe behind his with his gun out. Not to mention Joel the shotgun Joel had resting on the table.

"Yeah, I ain't from round here and these niggas be acting fool," he explained extracting the biggest .357 Kamari ever seen from the waist of his jeans. It seemed to take forever to get the barrel out.

"Damn money, is that joint big enough for you," he exclaimed with a smirk.

"It's like I said these niggas round here be acting fool but I know how to act fool right wit'em," he explained holding the gun by the handle and setting it down on a wall unit by the door before moving over to the coffee table where Kamari stood.

"How many you want?" Asked Joel from where he sat on the couch.

"I got eighteen hundred, how many you give me for that?" He asked pulling more money from his pocket.

"That'll get you 36 fifties, but Imma throw in three extras just because I like your attitude," interjected Kamari.

"Yeah, o.k." he said handing him the money as Joel begin to count out 39 fifties.

"Here you go," said Joel sliding his purchase across the table to him. Scooping them up he stuffed them into his pockets and turned to Kamari.

"Good looking slim. I be back to see yall again."

"We'll be here but do us a favor and leave the gun in your car," said Kamari looking him in the eye.

"You got that," he answered straight faced and walked over to the wall unit, picked up his gun, and tucked it away before leaving.

"Talking about a nigga being serious," laughed Joel.

"That's the attitude we gotta match out here," said Kamari, "right Abe."

"True dat."

"I gotta go take this girl back her car and get her to rent us some wheels. When I get the car Imma come back with more work cause I can see that's not gonna be enough."

"A'ight, here you go," said Joel handing him the money from the first package as Kamari passed him the money from the sell they'd just made.

"A'ight, we'll be back in an hour or two," he said as he and Knox headed out the door.

CHAPTER 64

As night fell on D.C. Kamari and Knox drove in the beige Dodge Caravan Tasheeva rented for them. They'd returned to the spot dropping of more work and were now in route to see Chew. Pulling up to a light on 14th and W Kamari spotted Chew standing out front a mom and pop store amongst a group of dudes, one of which was his god-brother. The light turned green and he pulled over parking across the street from them. He and Knox exited the Caravan receiving stares from the crowd as they proceeded across the street toward them. Even Chew who also noticed them crossing facial expression was difficult to discern. "Damn, what's up," exclaimed Kamari as they approached him.

"When did you get out here?" Chew asked walking toward them.

"Today. You remember Knox?"

"Yeah, what's up kid," he said with a nod. "So what you doing out here?"

"I got a spot out in South East."

"You better be careful it's wild over there. Over here is like Manhattan, but out there is like Brooklyn, a lot of shootings and shit."

254

"Yeah, that's what I'm hearing. But I made the trip with Brooklyn so I should be a'ight. What's up out here though, this how yall doing it," he remarked glancing around.

"Yeah, mostly everybody out here is from New York. We sell raw coke. We used to be up in Clifton Terrace but if niggas wasn't getting setup to be robbed, they were getting trapped off by jump-outs. So we moved down here and took it back to new York, the block."

"What's jump-outs?"

"That's what they call five-O out here because the way they jump out on niggas. So when you hear someone yell jump-outs you know what time it is. Yo, what's up with the Caravan, You got a family out here," he joked glancing over to were it was parked.

"I needed something with local tags that wouldn't draw no attention. And it's a lot of places to stash shit in there."

"Ok, I get it," he smiled as his god-brother called him. "Yeah, a'ight give me a minute," he answered. "Yo, let's hook up sometime. I be out here most nights so finding me won't be a problem."

"Yeah, I'll do that," Kamari replied as they slapped hands before he and Knox headed for the Caravan knowing him and Chew wouldn't be getting together no time soon. They'd grown apart in the years he'd been in D.C. he'd felt it immediately. He was an outsider to the life Chew had made for himself out here. The bond the streets of New York gave, the streets of D.C. had taken.

CHAPTER 65

Arriving at LaGuardia on an American Airlines shuttle from Washington D.C. Kamari dressed for a cooler New York weather wore a navy blue three quarter Polo windbreaker, Polo blue jeans, white Polo shirt, and a pair of white Polo sneakers. Walking beside him as they made their way through the crowded airport toward the exit was Knox who wasn't into the fashion thing. He kept it simple in a black Champion sweat pants; a white t-shirt, over which he wore a black Raiders windbreaker, and a pair of black Reebok classics. They'd finished the key of coke he'd brought out to D.C. in four days with no clientele making a little over forty-thousand, which in New York was unheard of. Joel being afraid to fly had taken half the money on the train with Abe who in working together in the spot had hit it off.

Outside the airport the day was cool and sunny, where limousines and Lincoln Town cars lined the entrance, their drivers holding cards displaying names, yellow cabs pulling up dropping off passengers and their luggage, rental car shuttles herding passengers off to their rental dealers, and baggage boys with their pulley carts hustling for tips. Everybody in a hurry to get somewhere or to get away from someplace, it was all a preview of the city that the airport provided access to.

Seeing a Chauffer standing next to a dark blue Lincoln Town car holding a card that simply read driver, they approached. "You waiting for someone?" Asked Kamari walking up to him.

"If you need a driver I'm your man," answered the driver a young Middle-Easterner.

"A'ight then let's go," said Kamari as the driver proceeded around to the driver-side. As Kamari open the back door for him and Knox to get in two casually dressed white men came out of nowhere flashing Federal badges on them.

"You fellas mind if we ask you a few questions," said one of the agents, his arm stretched out over the open car door blocking Kamari from getting inside. The second agent stood behind Knox sealing off any escape route.

"Sure, what's the problem?" Asked Kamari as the driver paused at the driver's door and stared over the hood of the car.

"There's no problem, we would just like to ask you a few questions, that's all."

"Well officer, agent sir, we're kinda in a hurry so if there's no problem than what's the purpose of you stopping us for questioning," he inquired staring over the open door at the agent who was a couple of inches shorter than him.

"Let's just say this is a random thing we do here at the airport. Now…"

"No. let's not just say anything. Especially when it violates our rights, so if there's no problem then we'll just be on our way like the rest of these good citizens around us," said Kamari cutting him off.

"In that case there is a problem," replied the agent as he slightly leaned in over the open door toward Kamari. "Your fucking mouth," he said in a near whisper. "Now step away from the car," he ordered directing them to the curb where his partner stood. Kamari just pursed him lips and nodded to Knocs before complying. Closing the Lincoln door the agent moved over to them pulling out a pen and pad. "Where are you two coming from?" He asked stopping in front of Kamari and staring down in his pad with his pen ready.

"Washington D.C.," answered Kamari.

"Do you have any identification on you?"

"No," they both answered.

"What are your names?"

"Anthony Roads," lied Kamari.

"Donnoven Terry," said Knox following his lead.

259

"What were you doing in Washington?" He asked addressing his question to Kamari with his eyes.

"Visiting my uncle."

"What's that in your pocket," he said pointing to a bulge in the pocket of Kamari's windsbreaker.

"Money," he answered without hesitation.

"Take it out and let me see," he directed watching as Kamari pulled out a three inch stack of bills wrapped with rubber bands.

"How much you got here?" He asked taking it and rifling through the bills which ranged from hundreds to tens.

"Ten thousand."

"Wow, that's a lot of money," he remarked glancing at his partner. "How about you?" he asked Knox who shook his head no even though he had another ten stuffed in the crotch of his sweats. "Empty your pockets," he ordered not believing him. "Both of you empty your pockets," he added. Complying they removed everything from their pockets as the agents patted them making sure they were empty. "Where did you get so much money, you rich?"

"No, my uncle sent that by me to my father on a business loan owed."

"If your not rich what are you doing getting into a limo," replied the agent.

"This ain't no limo, it's a cab," he said gesturing with his hand. "Yo, ain't this a cab," he yelled over to the driver who stood waiting.

"Yes, I'm cab driver," answered the driver receiving frowns from the agents. Turning back to Kamari the agent stared him knowing the money he held was drug money but there was nothing he could do. Having ten thousand in cash wasn't a crime, and most people didn't bring drugs to New York. They came to purchase them.

"Here you go," he said begrudgingly handing Kamari back the money. Taking it Kamari said nothing as he and Knox made their way to the Lincoln climbing in back as the driver got in behind the wheel and pulled off.

Exiting LaGuardia on the Flushing side the driver made a right toward the B.Q.E. Kamari who had been watching the rearview mirror since pulling noticed a light blue Crown Victorian with four agents tailing them. Two of which were the ones who stopped and questioned them. "They following us," he announced.

"I know, I see them," replied the driver as he turned onto the B.Q.E.

"Go to Manhattan," said Kamari glancing in the mirror.

"Fucking faggots, don't got nothing better to do," cursed Knox pulling the money from the crotch of his sweats and placing it in the pocket of his windbreaker.

"I didn't even see the other two, they musta been parked somewhere watching us the whole time," remarked Kamari as the driver switched off onto the Grand Central Expressway with the agents imitating his every move. "Is this your first time being followed by the feds?" Kamari asked the driver.

"Yes, I believe so," he answered glancing in the mirror.

"Well your doing a good job," he smiled as the driver switched off onto the 59th Street Bridge coming out onto 2nd Avenue in mid-town with the light blue Crown Victorian nowhere in sight.

"I believe we lost them," announced the driver excitedly smiling.

"Ok, drive around for a few just to be sure then go to the Gucci Shop on 57th. I wanna get a few things before we head home," replied Kamari with a smile.

CHAPTER 66

Inside Shelley's bedroom Kamari sat on her bed eating a plate of fried fish, yams, black-eye peas and rice with cornbread. Her mother had prepared a send off dinner for the oldest of her two sisters who was visiting from Florida with her two children. "I need some hot sauce," he said putting a piece of fish in his mouth.

"Why didn't you tell me when I was fixing your plate?" She asked eyeing with a pouting frown.

"Cause I wasn't thinking about it," he answered smiling at her as she sucked her teeth. He watched as she proceeded to the closed door with her long stocking clad legs spilling out from under the navy blue and gray plaid knee high skirt she wore, into a pair of navy blue leather loafers. Her hair which hung drape down the back of her off white blouse swayed slightly with the rhythm of her petite hips as she open the door and left the room. Kamari and her's was the most open of relationships. She never questioned him upon his returns after being gone sometimes for months at a time. On one of his returns he'd been gone so long he felt the need to ask her if she was seeing someone. Offended, she'd sucked her teeth saying that nobody could ever come between them. The only thing she asked of him was that he never get another woman pregnant. Loving children the way she did always helping her mother who ran a day-care look after other peoples' children. She couldn't stand the thought of a child of his by another woman being the object of her animosity. To him it was a flattering glimpse into her hopes for a future with him.

"Here, you go," she said returning and setting the hot sauce on the tray-stand beside his plate as she closed the door.

"Thanks," he replied as she sat down next to him. "Your mother put a lot of love into this," he said dumping hot sauce on what was left of his fish and greens.

"Dagg, you got enough," she exclaimed smiling at him as she caressed his back.

"What, food?"

"No. Hot sauce," she said laughing and making him laugh too. "How's Ski," she inquired of his cousin who was with him when they met at a party in Yonkers.

"He's a'ight," he answered setting his fork down on the now empty plate and downing what remained of his glass of water.

"Let me take this to the kitchen," she said getting up removing everything from the tray. Minutes later she returned with a dish cloth and wiped down the tray-stand before taking it away.

"Your too good to me, you know that," when she returned closing the door behind her and smiling over at him.

"I'm just happy to see you that's all," she replied sitting down beside him. "I missed you, didn't you miss me,' she said grinning seductively placing her hand beneath his shirt making circles with her long natural nails on his bare back.

"You know I did," he answered, the sensation of her nails running across his back along with the direction of the conversation stimulating him both mentally and physically.

"Knowing and hearing is two different things," she exclaimed leaning over kissing him on the neck as he sat staring ahead at the closed door.

"I miss you too," he smiled as she nibbled on his ear lobe while running her nails across his back which was a stirring combination that gave her his full attention.

"Come on let's do it," she breathed in his ear, her words making his already inflated member jump.

"Nahhh, you crazy," he laughed. "Your family is in the next room."

"So what, they're not going to come in here, my door is closed," she explained reaching between his legs taking hold of the bulge in his pants.

"Yo, chill," he exclaimed reluctantly pushing her hand away. "You can't even lock your door."

"Come on Kamari, how you going to tell me no," she pouted ignoring him as she reached for his belt buckle and begin tugging on it loose.

"A'ight, a'ight, hold up," he said laughing at how determine she was, a side of her he'd never seen before. "Look, if we do it, we gotta do it by the door so if anyone comes you can stop them at the door."

"I don't care, let's just do it," she replied grinning mischievously standing up and kicking off her shoes.

"Look at you," he laughed watching as she slid down her panties and stepping out of them.

"What," she said coyly smiling as she leaned over him and stuffed her panties in the pocket of his jeans. "Something to keep me on your mind," she whispered taking him by the hand from the bed over to the door. Placing her back against the door she begin kissing him as she undid his belt and let his pants drop down to his ankles. Reaching into his boxers she freed his erection and began caressing her hand up and down the length of it as she slid down to a squatting position until her face was level with it. Slowly she ran her tongue around the bulging head of his dick as she stared up at him with wanting eyes before enveloping him in the wet warmth of her mouth.

"Damn," breathed Kamari as she slowly ascended on his shaft inch by inch drawing back only when she could go no further leaving a sheen of saliva coating on his dick as she caressed the head with her full lips. She repeated this process several times. Unable to take it any longer Kamari quickly pulled her up by her shoulders and hiked her skirt up around her waist. Palming her firm buttocks he lifted her into the air as she grabbed hold around his neck with one hand and firmly took hold of his pulsating brick hard dick with the other. Slightly bending his knees he allowed her an angle as she guided him inside of her dripping moist pussy.

"Yeah, ahhhh," she exhaled as he pushed his way further inside of her. Sliding his hand from her buttocks to her thighs he lifted her higher and filled her completely with one big upward thrust as she wrapped both arms around his neck. "Mmmm, yes Kamariii," she cried softly pulling herself closer to him burying her face in his neck, biting him lightly as she bounced up and down needing to feel him deep inside of her.

"Shhh, don't make so much noise," he whispered bucking his hips to meet her downward motion.

"Stop worrying, ahhh," she moaned, her voice heavy with lust.

"Shelly," came a child's voice from outside the door.

"Oh shit," cursed Kamari freezing in motion.

"Don't stop that's my nephew," she whispered to him as he started to put her down. "What is it," she called out as Kamari held her in mid-air.

"Nanna said do you want some desert?"

"Maybe later," she answered.

"Ok," replied her nephew and they could hear him turn and walk away.

"You know you crazy, right," grinned Kamari as he begin moving again.

"Onlyyy…for you babyyy," she moaned downing the sounds of her pleasure by burying her face in the knape of his neck as he picked up his pace.

"Ahhh, yeah," he groaned through clenched teeth trying to wait on her as he felt his beeper vibrating in his jean pocket.

"Mmmm…yesss..that's it Kamariii…," she moaned burying her face deeper in his neck and locked her legs around his waist drawing him inside of her as she grind to a shuddering climax. In that same instant Kamari exploded inside of her adding to her rolling climax. Standing still he remained holding her as the waves of their pleasures subsided. Recovering before him she began planting soft wet kisses on his neck up to his ears whispering sexual promises to him.

"That's it," he said feeling himself begin to rise inside of her.

"You are such a scary cat," she teased smiling as he set her down.

"How when I just gave it to you with your whole family in the next room," he grinned pulling up his pants.

"Whatever," she laughed pulling a wash cloth from a dresser drawer.

"Yeah I know whatever," he came back checking to see who beeped him. "Oh, I have to go," he announced as he stared at the coded number which belonged to his cousin Pudder they were ready for him at his Aunt Bev's.

CHAPTER 67

"What's up, yall ready," exclaimed Kamari to Pudder and Ski who both were seated at the kitchen table as he entered carrying a bag containing two keys of coke he'd cooked up at his apartment.

"We waiting on you," smiled Pudder as Ski fiddled with a digital scale on the table.

"Where's Bev," he inquired setting the bag off coke down on the table.

"She went out somewhere," answered Pudder. "You know uncle Sweet Water up her from Jersey."

"Nah, where he at?"

"Probably downstairs at Momma's" interjected Ski.

"Yall, go ahead and get started. I gotta use the bathroom," he said turning away from them.

"How you want us to do it," Ski called after him.

"Pudder knows," he yelled back hurrying down the hall to the bathroom pushing the door open not realizing it was occupied. "What the fuck is you doing," he said staring at his uncle Sweet Water sitting on top the toilet bowl, leaning forward with his left arm placed between his crossed legs, a strap tied around his bicep, one end clenched between his teeth, and a syringe needle in his right hand as he stared up at him.

"Hey where you put the razors," asked Pudder approaching Kamari.

"Come on, I'll show you," he said quickly shutting the bathroom door before he reached him.

"What's the matter with you," asked Pudder observing the expression on his face as he passed him to the kitchen, but getting no answer.

"There right up here," he exclaimed taking a box of razors down from one of the cabinet shelves and handing them to him. Moving over to the table where Ski was weighing out eigths he checked the scale. "Make sure yall get a hundred fifties or better of each eighth," he explained as Sweet Water entered the kitchen.

"Kamari, let me have a word with you," he asked turning and leading the way from the kitchen as Kamari followed.

"What's wrong with you using that shit," angrily questioned Kamari once they reached the next room.

"I don't do this all the time."

"It's the fact that you do it at all. You can get that shit fucking around like that," he said realizing that this was probably no doubt his reason for being in New York and not Jersey with his family.

"I use my own works," protested Sweet Water pulling them from his pocket in a small black pouch.

"I never knew you fucked around like that," he frowned shaking his head as he stared down at the content of the pouch his uncle displayed in defense of addiction. As if having his own needle made it all right. It was the same dope fiend mannerism he'd when Kamari opened the bathroom door on him. He hadn't tried to conceal or explain. He'd just waited for him to shut the door so that he could continue what he was doing. "I'm through with it," he said having dealt with enough fiends to know that there was nothing he could say or do that would change what his uncle had become. He didn't even know when it had happened. "If that's what you wanna do, it's on you. Just do that shit in here no more, suppose Pudder or one of them would of walked in on you? And get that shit outta here," he said pointing at the black pouch.

"Your right nephew," he replied somewhat ashamed that he had to hear this from his sisters son who was some twenty years his junior. "I hear your out in D.C.," he said as Kamari started to walk away.

"Yeah," he replied not in the mood for idle conversation with him after what he'd just witnessed which shattered all respect he had for him. Something his uncle recognized in his eyes and in the tone in which he spoke.

"We have family out there, you know," he added getting his attention.

"Yeah, we do," he replied now interested in what he had to say.

"Sure do, you have a cousin out there around your age, name Brandon. He was into some things the last time I was out there."

"Introduce me to him," he directed more than asked.

"Heck yeah, that's your family," he smiled. "I'll even go out there with you if you want me to," he continued trying to redeem what he'd lost.

"Yeah, we can do that," he answered figuring he could send him ahead with the coke and the advantages working through family in D.C. It offered all kinds of promising possibilities.

CHAPTER 68

"Here you are," announced the Ethiopian cab driver who at National Airport Had been reluctant to accept Kamari and Knox as passengers once they gave their destination. It was only after paying in advance and an assurance that they meant him no ill intent that he'd agreed to take them. "Ok, ok, I have to go now," urged the driver rushing them from his cab.

"Can we get our things," replied Kamari showing patients.

"I don't like it here. I tell you this," he said glancing around out the windows.

"Its broad day light, ain't nobody gonna do nothing to you," remarked Knox gathering his bags as Kamari opened the door shaking his head at the ridiculousness of the drivers' behavior.

"This is why I no like dealing with you people," complained the driver.

"Shut the fuck up, you should of stayed your scared as in Africa," responded Knox as they exited the cab. "Yeah, Yeah, fuck you to," he continued talking over the driver and leaving the door open as the driver complained in his native tongue.

274

"He needs to switch occupations," laughed Kamari watching as the driver who was so afraid pulled off with the door open leaving them standing on 1500 and Congress in South East, which was smack in the middle of a high crime area of D.C. Proceeding over to the two story housing complex where he was to meet SweetWater and the relatives he hadn't know he had in D.C. he observed a group of dudes hustling on a corner. He smiled at life's dark humor imagining that if he was to visit all the family he had in the world, he'd find them in similar places across the globe. This being the case in New York and here in D.C. for it seemed to be the lot that was his and his descendants in life. A life of poverty, struggle, dismay, and limitations, but he'd rather welcome death than accept any of it. Reaching the door he rang the bell and several seconds later it was opened by a light skinned woman that resembled his aunt Bev. A resemblance that made him smile.

"Gregory, is this your nephew standing here on my doorstep," she yelled addressing SweetWater by his given name, returning Kamari's smile as she stared through the screen door at him.

"Yeah that's Kamari," confirmed SweetWater appearing in the doorway behind the woman who was about his age, early 40's.

"I'm your momma's first cousin Gloria and your second," she declared. "Now yall get on in here," she smiled opening the screen door for them. "And whose your friend?" She asked glancing at Knox as they entered.

"I'm Knocs miss," he answered coming to a stop just inside the door.

"Come on here now, what y'all stopping here for. My home is your home," she fussed ushering them into an adjoining room as SweetWater followed behind her grinning with a drink in hand. Inside the room on a sofa sat a cute light-skinned female about Kamari's age who Gloria introduced as her sister's daughter and his cousin Valerie.

"Your cousin Brandon will be back shortly. He went to drop his girlfriend off," she said as he and Knox took a seat on the sofa next to Valerie. "Y'all want something to drink?"

"Nah, I'm a'ight," replied Kamari wanting to get SweetWater alone and find out about his two keys of coke.

"I'm good," said Knox.

"Well, if y'all want anything just help yourselves," she said sitting on the arm of a love seat in which sat SweetWater, holding his glass of alcoholic beverage. "Now, which one of my cousins is your momma?"

"Joanne's his mother Gloria. I told you that earlier," said SweetWater as Kamari looked on realizing they'd might of both had too much to drink.

"Shit it's so many of them. Where my drink at," she said looking around.

"Here you go," said Valarie passing her a glass off the end table.

"Thank you, Valerie baby," she said turning back to Kamari. "I ain't seen your momma in years, how is she," she asked picking up where she left off.

"Oh, she's doing fine," he answered.

"Here is Brandon," she announced as her son entered the room and they all turned to look. "Come on over here and meet your cousin Kamari," she said pointing at him as Brandon walked over and stood beside her. Brandon who had a muscular build, stood six even. He wore his hair cut low and sharply trimmed as was the goatee he sported. Dressed in blue jeans, T-shirt, and a pair of Travel Fox, his presence over shadowed everyone in the room as they sat.

"What's happening," he said shaking Kamari then Knox hand as they introduced themselves. "How long y'all been here?"

"They just got here about 20 some odd minutes ago," answered his mother making Kamari laugh. "Whoops, I wasn't supposed to answer that," she said placing a hand over her mouth as Brandon frowned at her.

"You'll want to get out of here?" He asked with a smirk.

"Where can we put our stuff?" asked Kamari.

"I'll take care of your bags," said SweetWater handing Gloria his drink as he got up from his seat.

"A'ight, and let me speak to you outside for a minute," Kamari said as they followed Brandon out the house.

Out front the house the four of them stood. "Everything straight with that?" Kamari asked speaking to SweetWater who was standing beside him.

"O'yeah, I got it. You want it right now?"

"Nah, give me a few minutes," he said figuring he'd call Tasheeva to come and pick it up. "All right, I'm going to be inside. When you're ready, just let me know," he said, going back into the house.

"Gregory was telling me that y'all been out here getting it," said Brandon standing to Kamari's left.

"Yeah, but we ain't been out here that long, a little over a week if that."

"What strip y'all on?"

"Strip," repeated Kamari the use of the word lost on him for second. "Oh you mean-"

"Where y'all working out of," finished his cousin.

"On Mellon and Newcomb."

"Y'all right here in Southeast."

"Gregory told me that you used to fuck around," said Kamari.

"Yeah, I was getting it at one time, Joe. But I've got busted and found out that jail ain't it. I did 18 months on the farm and called it a wrap."

"The farm, what's that?"

"The youth center down Lorton Virginia. It's near a dairy farm, so that's what we call it. It's wild as shit down there joe."

"How old are you?" Kamari asked not interested in hearing about no prison.

"Twenty three, and you."

"Nineteen," he answered. "Well if you don't fuck around than..."

"Ay, I don't," he replied cutting him off. "But most my folk do. So don't trip you family. I'mma see that you meet who you need to meet, and know who you need to know. I got you joe," he said grinning.

"A'ight," smiled Kamari. "What I need to know right now is two things."

"Shoot Joe."

"What is them dudes over their selling?" He asked nodding towards the dudes standing on the corner.

"Bone, that's a bone strip."

"Huh, what's bone?"

"Heroin, dope joe," he answered smiling.

"Second, why you keep calling me Joe," smiled back Kamari."Y'all say yo, we say Joe. It's slaing cousin dat all," he answered, and they all laughed as Kamari concluded he was going to enjoy hanging out with his cousin.

CHAPTER 69

Kamari sat in a chair inside Brandon's room lacing up the high-top black Gucci sneakers listening to Knox who stood in the doorway of the room. He was telling him about Tasheeva's roommate who he'd been messing around with since arriving in D.C. A week had passed since meeting his cousin who true to his word had Kamari running around the chocolate city building ties. He introduced him to dealers in North East, Northwest, and all over the South East. Some of whom Kamari had hit with G-packs on a 30-70 split by agreeing to sell them ounces for eight hundred when he brought in his next package; which he planned to double each time. "Where she from again," asked Kamari sitting up.

"Chicago," answered Knox.

"A Windy City cutie, huh," he replied rising to his feet checking himself out, in the Gucci hightops, a pair of prewashed jeans, and a black short sleeve shirt with red stripes that Tasheeva picked out for him in Georgetown. "So what you tell her?"

"Yo, I ain't tell her nothing," he exclaimed grinning.

"You told or did something to her cause Tasheeva says she's driving her crazy talking about you."

281

"Yo, I'm telling you I ain't doing nothing," Knox laughed. "I ain't into that my girl shit. I giv'em some rough dick and keep it moving."

"Well that did it, she must ain't never had no rough dick," Kamari said laughing with him as they went into the living room where SweetWater and Gloria sat, drinks and in hand running their mouths.

"How you feeling Kamari?" Asked Gloria in reference to the day before when he'd been sick and throwing up.

"Better. I think it came from flying back and forth. The change of climate and whatnot," he answered as him and Knox stood before them.

"The way you been sleeping around here you'll might have some girl running around pregnant," she frowned at SweetWater.

"Shit we been calling your mother grandma for so many years she won't mind," smiled Sweetwater.

"No, it ain't nothing like that," he replied with a smile thinking about Natasha back in New York.

"Yall ready to get up out of here," said Brandon emerging from the kitchen eating a hot dog.

CHAPTER 70

The club scene in D.C. was much different from that of New York. The crowds were less pretentious in demeanor. Almost everyone took to the floor, hooting and hollering, stepping to the music, unafraid to sweat and have a good time; the roar of the crowd rivaling that of the music which was nothing like the music played in New York clubs. The music of choice in D.C. was called Go-Go. A lively form of music driven by heavy base lines, horns, and drums so wild in rhythm and array that the affect on club goers was almost ritual like. Sitting in the midst of all this Kamari felt the urge to partake but he wasn't there to party. He was there for a lesson of whose who on the streets of the nations capital, and Brandon was his tutor. Together with Knox they spent the night nursing their drinks while casually observing as well as meeting a few of these individuals; those who Brandon knew personally.

Across the street from the club as it was letting out Kamari and Knocs stood with Brandon in front of his black Toyota Four-Runner talking as a dude Brandon had introduced them to earlier pulled up alongside of them in a white BMW 540 accompanied by a female. "Hey what's happin' joe. We goin do dat or what," he yelled through the passenger window as he leaned over the female.

"Yeah, hold on joe," replied Brandon turning to Kamari. "You want to get with main man on what we talked about?"

"Yeah, we can do that. Set it up for next week," he answered referring to an even exchange between him and the dude who controlled the bone strip around Brondon's way.

"Ok," replied Brandon walking over to the BMW.

"Yo, look at this shit," said Knox nodding toward what looked like two females in a red 325 BMW laughing and joking with a few dudes.

"Ain't that…"

"Yup, two niggas dressed like bitches."

"Yo, that's craziness right there," exclaimed Kamari watching as the dudes conversed and socialized with the two like they were really females. "You think they know," he said unbelievingly.

"If we can tell from here they gotta know," replied Knox as Brandon rejoined them.

"A'ight joe, it's taken care of and I got some folk on P street to give it to when you get it."

"Yo, what's up with that scene over there?" asked Kamari pointing with his eyes.

"Oh, that's peoples, they gettin' it too," answered Brandon laughing at the expression on Kamari's face. "Yall seen enough or yall wanna hang out awhile longer," he joked.

"Yeah, cousin we definitely seen enough," replied Kamari shaking his head as they proceeded to leave when the sudden sounds of gunshots clapped like thunder. They quickly dropped into squatting positions beside the truck as the sound of females screaming could be heard amidst the gun fire. Glancing about as he held onto the handle of the passenger door Kamari could see people fleeing the front of the club as a dude clutching his blood spewing stomach stumbled out into the street followed by another with a gun in hand who fired several more shots that sent the dude to the ground in a jittery motion.

"Come on, get in joe," yelled Brandon who had slid behind the wheel of the truck during all the commotion as a dark colored 300Z flew past them and came to a screeching stop beside the gunman who jumped in through open T-top roof as the driver peeled off in a cloud of smoke.

Kamari and Knox climbed into the truck and Brandon pulled off driving toward the dude laid out in the middle of the street. As they passed Kamari noticed a gun in his hand as

285

he laid bleeding to death, his blood forming a puddle as cold as the steel of the gun he held in his lifeless hand.

CHAPTER 71

"Kamari," whispered Tasheeva in the dark of her room tapping him on the back as he laid sound asleep in her bed at the condo she shared with her roommate. Leaving tomorrow for New York he'd spent much of the day with her shopping and hanging out. They'd even gone out to Maryland and visited Monique. Seeing her, Kamari couldn't keep from comparing the life she now lived to that of the one she lived when they'd met in at the strip club in New York. It was a three-hundred and sixty-degree turn around he'd though as he'd watched her child. "Kamari," Tasheeva called again shaking him.

"Huh," he mumbled stirring a bit.

"Your pager," she replied.

"What," he said opening his eyes as he rolled over to face her.

"Your pager is going off."

"Oh," he said hearing it vibrating on the night-stand next to him. Picking it up he checked the number, it was Joel. Grabbing the phone he sat it on the bed beside him and dialed the number. Tasheeva snuggled up next to him and placed her head on his chest, the warmth of her nakedness a welcomed comfort. "What's happening," he said into the phone his voice deep with sleep.

"What you was sleeping? ," asked Joel on the other end.

"Yeah I'm up now, what's up?"

"We need a refill," he answered to the sound of music playing in the background.

"What's that noise?"

"Music, a head was selling a stereo and cassette-player so I copped it. You know; needed some music up in here."

"Yeah a'ight, what time is it?"

"Five to two."

"A'ight, Imma bring half the usual. That should hold yall until the morning."

"That"ll work."

"A'ight see you in a few," said Kamari hanging up and staring down at Tasheeva, who had fallen back to sleep as she hugged up on him. She'd wanted to make the trip with him back to New York but he didn't want her to get involved in his business beings that he was intimate with her. Females

288

were too unpredictable when they fell in love, especially if scorned. This he'd witnessed first-hand with his aunts and their girlfriends. Her involvement now was only temporary until he could establish a full set-up out there. Besides in New York there was no time or place for her. He had to re-up and arrange for a less risky method for the increase in product he planned to bring in with each trip. He also had to recruit more workers to give Joel and Abe some leisure. Then on top of all that there was still Erica, Ameina, and Shelly all of whom would be vying for his time. "Tasheeva," he called waking her.

"Mmmm," she answered.

"I gotta make a run."

"No Booo," she groaned snuggling up to him even tighter.

"I'll be back," he said sliding out from under her and going into the bathroom in the nude. Coming out minutes later he found her with the light on laying sideways on her elbow watching him and he was overcome with a sense of déjà vu that made him smile.

"What you smiling at?" She asked returning his smile.

"Nah, I just had a feeling of déjà vu," he answered stepping into a pair of boxers.

"Yeah, I bet you did. All the girls you done left in the middle of the night like this," she teased with a smirk as she watched him dress.

"Where your car keys?" he asked ignoring her as he slipped on his shirt.

"Over here," she said grabbing them from the nightstand and tossing them to him. Catching them he walked over to a closet where in the back on the floor he retrieved one of her shoe boxes. Inside was what remained of the two keys. Taking a hundred pack of fifties he stuffed them down in his jeans and turned to leave.

"I'll see you in a few," he said opening and shutting the bedroom door behind him as she turned off the light and laid down to sleep. Proceeding down the hall to the living-room he smiled at the sight of Knox and Tasheeva's roommate entangled on carpeted floor, their blankets barley covering their nakedness. Laughing he recalled their conversation earlier in the week and decided to leave him sleeping as he headed for the door.

CHAPTER 72

Unable to sleep Joanne laid in bed staring up at the ceiling, her husband snoring beside her. This was the case most nights when she thought about her son and what he was involved in out on the streets. Every ringing phone in the middle of the night brought on her worst fears. On this night she felt a strong sense of dread surrounding her thoughts of him. Getting out of bed being careful not to wake her husband, she slipped her bare feet into her slippers and in her nightgown, a scarf on her head she left the room.

Entering the dining room turning on the light she walked over to an old china cabinet. Reaching up on top of it she took down some old family photo albums. Carrying them over to the table she sat and glanced up at a clock on the wall showing twenty after two. Opening one of the photo albums she began flipping through the pages until she came to a photo of her son that was one of her favorites.

It was the earliest photo she had of him, all his earlier photos having been destroyed in a fire that had almost claimed his life as an infant. Looking at the photo she smiled. He was no more than two years old at the time standing in front of a fully decorated Christmas tree. He had on a beige and brown plaid wool coat with matching hat she'd gotten that Christmas for him, smiling brightly for the camera. A smile as promising as his birth which had brought her such hope

291

for the future and the joys he would bring to her life. She found it difficult to turn the page but she did coming to a photo of him that made her laugh away the tears in her eyes.

She remembered the day like it was yesterday. His uncle had taken the photo. He was sitting in a chair he'd placed at the top of the stairs in the center of his grandmother's weathered porch. Only six years old at the time he had made his uncle wait while he set everything up. Than like a professional he'd posed, seated with one hand resting on his thigh, elbow propped on his knee trying to look serious like the statue of the thinking man he'd seen at a museum days earlier. He had a full afro of knotty hair on his head that he wouldn't let anybody comb but his grandmother; and even then she had to wet it first. He was always the thinker searching for easy and better ways of doing things she thought turning to the next page.On it she found a photo of him at his six grade graduation that brought back memories of all the trouble he'd gotten into in school before reaching that point, and all that would follow. Gone from his eyes were the innocents of the previous photos. He seemed more conscious of his surroundings and himself she thought remembering the British Walkers he wore in the photo and how she'd brought them using some of the rent money. The expression on his face brought back the feeling of dread that had forced her from bed. He appeared to be consumed by his thoughts, his face bearing tad-tell signs of tension that pained her heart because no one so young should have been burdened by their thoughts. And with this revelation tears begin to fall from her eyes because she was noticing now what she should have noticed back then and now it might be too late. "God Almighty I beg you, please have mercy on my son's soul," she cried bowing her head, her eyes shut tight as she prayed for the little boy she'd lost along the way. Her tears falling on Kamari's six grade photo.

CHAPTER 73

Out front the house on Newcomb police and ambulances sat parked. There flashing lights casting on the neighborhood like search lights. At the entrance of the gate leading up to the house laid Abe, who had crawled from the house judging from the trail of blood smeared on the ground from it to where he was laid dead. Inside the apartment the blood ran even thicker where police found three more victims. One of which was Joel lying on the floor of the living-room fighting for his life as paramedics worked feverishly to contain the bleeding of multiple gunshot wounds to his torso. Across from him lying dead in the doorway of the kitchen as homicide detectives and police stepped over him to search the rest of the apartment was Norm. He'd been shot once in the back of the head. Not far from him behind the open door of the apartment was the most gruesome of the three. Propped up against the wall in a sitting position where he'd came to rest after being propelled into the wall by a shotgun blast that shredded his face placing half his brains and head on the wall before a second blast in the neck left what remained of his head hanging by mangled flesh on his chest. Having seen enough a detective covered the unidentifiable victim with a crime scene blanket.

Back outside a plain clothed officer escorting a hysterically crying Sophia from the house in route to his patrol car was stopped by another wearing a blue wind-breaker with the letters D.E.A in yellow on back. Standing beside them Sophia couldn't believe that Norm was dead as she scanned the faces of on lookers, many of whom were her neighbors and fellow addicts. She wondered if any of them had some rock they could spare. She was in need of a hit bad, having not had a chance to get her share before gunshots sent her scurrying under the bed where the police found her. The plain clothed detective handed Sophia over to the D.E.A agent who tapped her on the elbow indicating it was time to go. Kamari was standing among the crowd watching as she was placed in a car and driven away. He then jumped into Tasheeva's car thinking it was time to leave D.C.

CHAPTER 74

Rolling out of the parking lot of White Castle onto Boston Road, in a red Volkswagen Cabriolet and followed by a white one, their tops down, Kamari, with Mink seated beside him, sped down the road, catching as many lights as he could. Knox and Stan trailed closely behind in the white Cabriolet before coming to a stop at a red light. It was a little after four in the afternoon, and they were returning from downtown, where they had done some shopping and drove around from Manhattan to the Bronx meeting females. With over two hundred thousand dollars in cash spread out among three safes, the majority of which he kept in a safe at his aunt Stacey's, and another recently placed at Marco's, Kamari felt he'd come far enough to have a little fun especially after DC. He'd been back in New York for two weeks and the details of what happened were still unclear. All he knew was that Joel was in a coma. Through Blass he arranged for Joel's family to travel out to D.C. and be by his side. Other than that business was good in New York. He was now getting ten bricks at a time, all on consignment. Elias had come down on the price and refused to take any money from him up front, saying he was familía.

During this period he and Knox built a bond much like the one between him and Mink. Unlike Mink, Knox was more open with him, discussing his feelings about everything from family and women to death. He valued Kamari's opinion and confided in him for advice. He told him about his family back in England and what it was like over there. Kamari told him that he always wanted to go over there to shop for leathers, and that one day they would go together and he could visit his family. There were other conversations between them, dark in nature and somber in tone.

Knox would tell him that if there was such a place as hell, he knew it would be his final resting place. This he always said with a grin, but his eyes held the seriousness of his words; the grin was a mask. Kamari would try to persuade him from these thoughts, but he remained convinced in what for him had become a belief. Therefore, whenever he would bring it up, Kamari would ignore him until he changed the subject. Kamari came into the game facing death, and though he had walked away with his life, its presence remained forever present as he descended deeper into the life despite his efforts to walk away from it.

However, the incident that, for Kamari, solidified their bond was a recent trip out to New Jersey to look into putting work in the projects with the kid from out there, whom Cush introduced him to. Kamari and Knox had been standing in front of one of the project buildings, while the kid went inside to get one of the dudes he would be working with, when a group of dudes approached them with a shotgun drawn and asked what they were doing out there. Kamari gave the kid's name and explained that they were waiting for him. Satisfied, the group turned and began to walk away, until one of them shouted, "Let's take their jackets," referring to the designer leathers they wore. The one with the shotgun responded by turning the shotgun on them again. Without hesitation, Knox grabbed the barrel and punched him in the face, as he yelled out for Kamari to run, and he did the same.

Kamari took off in one direction and Knox in the direction where the car was parked, which was inside the projects. Kamari had run about a block before realizing the group with the shotgun had gone after Knox and not him. Turning around, he headed back to the projects for Knox. When he reached the mouth of the projects parking lot, Knox and the kid they had came with skirted out and skidded to a stop in front of him. The kid jumped into the front seat, and they pulled off. In the back seat, Knox sat removing what was left of his shirt, his leather jacket gone.

"You a'ight?" Kamari asked, noticing he had lost one of his sneakers.

The kid was saying something as to the identity of those in the group while he drove. However, all Kamari heard was what Knox said to him as he sat shirtless in the back seat.

"Yo, I'm just glad they came after me and not you."

That statement, though it wasn't meant to, made Kamari feel uncomfortable, because although he had and would go to bat for his peoples, he had never actually placed or thought about placing himself in harm's way to spare someone else. As he stared at Knox in the back seat, back scraped up from falling on the ground, removing the single sneaker from his foot, for the first in his life, Kamari thought lowly of himself in comparison to another human being.

Continuing down Boston Road, they drove into the Vernon and made for the block. Arriving, they parked across the street from Big Al's, where Blass stood amongst the usual crowd with Rings. Getting out, they proceeded over to them.

"Yo, what's up with the White Castle?" shouted Blass, seeing Kamari with a cup of soda and Mink and Stan eating burgers and onion rings as they crossed the street.

"Go ahead. It's a whole bag of shit in the car," said Kamari, as they stepped onto the curb.

"Bring enough back for me," Rings yelled out to Blass as he made his way across the street to the car.

"Just bring the whole bag," added Kamari.

"I can't stand this bitch right here," exclaimed Stan, referring to a brown-complexioned female in a denim miniskirt, who was heading their way. "Hay, Knox, smack this bitch for me. I hate this bitch," he added loud enough for her to hear as she neared.

"Smack her for what?" Knox asked, turning his mouth up at him.

Being around them, Kamari had noticed how Stan would use Knox to do his dirty work, which most of the time, would be something stupid like what he'd just asked.

"Cause I don't like her," he answered, as Blass returned with the bag of White Castle.

"Well, you smack her then," Knox replied, taking Kamari's advice to let Stan do his own dirty work.

To this, Stan said nothing. He just watched as the female passed and rolled her eyes at him.

"What's wrong with you?" asked Kamari, while looking over at Mink, who kept sniveling and messing with his nose.

"Allergies," he answered, moving his hand away from his nose quickly.

"Yo, you heard from Joel's mother?" Kamari asked Blass, who was gulping down burgers like a seagull.

"Yeah, he's still in the coma and they got him hand cuffed to the bed with police guards at his door, but their not telling her nothing." Kamari just shook his head, he'd played it a thousand ways in his head but still the only way to find out what happed that night was from Joel.

"So it's a waiting game," he said for a lack of better words. Blass nodded in silence.

"Drop me off at my crib to get my bike," said Mink, talking to Stan, who stood beside him.

"Yeah, I got you. Knox, what's up for later?" Stan asked.

"I'm going out to Brooklyn tonight, but I'll be back in the morning," Knox replied.

"A'ight, I'll see you then, if I don't see you later. Mink, you ready?"

Without saying a word to anyone, Mink followed Stan to the car and they left. Kamari took all of this in as another example of Mink's strange behavior.

"Oh yeah, Kamari," said Rings. "Your man Jamaican Calvin got murdered."

"Get the fuck outta here!" he said, not believing it.

"Word, somebody shot him in the head out in Texas."

"Damn," Kamari said, shaking his head as he recalled the last time he seen him, and him trying to get Kamari to go out to Texas with him.

"Who's that? Do I know him?" asked Knox.

"Nah, you never met him," answered Kamari, thinking that he never would. "So you straight?"

"Yeah," said Blass. "And Mink's girl Shonda was looking for you," he added.

"When was this?"

"Like a half an hour ago. She said she was heading home."

"A'ight, I'ma see y'all later," he said, deciding he'd head over to Shonda's, who probably wanted to see him about the situation with her and Mink.

CHAPTER 75

Stationed outside of Shonda's apartment, Kamari could hear music emanating from inside while he waited for someone to answer the door. When nobody answered, he gave the door three slow, hard knocks, making sure he'd be heard this time. The music went off, and seconds later, Shonda opened the door holding a baby in her arm.

"Oh, I see you got my message. Come in," she said, holding the door open as he stepped inside. "Have a seat," she offered, closing the door and leading the way into the living room.

Taking a seat on the sofa, he watched as she sat down beside him, placing the baby on her lap. She carried her pregnancy well, he thought, not putting on too much weight that he could see. She wore a white shirt that was several sizes bigger than she normally wore to accommodate her condition, along with a pair of red terrycloth sweats. Her face glowed with the vibrancy of the life she carried inside of her, giving her chocolate skin a serene look as she sat there with her hair going back in cornrows, the fire in her eyes that had drawn Mink to her like a moth to a flame still burning strong.

"Whose baby?" he asked.

"Tammy's. I'm babysitting. Getting some practice, you know," she replied, smiling.

"When are you due?"

"Late October."

"Everything cool as far as the process?" he asked, having seen enough of his aunts have babies to know that it was no walk in the park.

"Yeah, everything is fine," she answered.

"So what did you wanna talk to me about?"

"It's not about Mink not wanting nothing to do with me and the baby," she said, then paused as she felt the sting of voicing her reality.

"Nah, it's not like that. I spoke to him. He's just afraid that he doesn't have what it takes to be a father. He'll come around once the baby is born. Watch what I tell you," he said, hoping that would be the case because Mink had told him no such thing.

In fact, when Kamari tried to talk to him about it, he outright refused to acknowledge the situation.

"Like I said, that's not what I wanted to talk to you about," she replied, knowing Mink would never admit to being afraid of anything. "I saw Dave the other day."

"What's up with him? I haven't seen him in awhile. He ain't been the same since Staggs died."

"He's doing all right, but him and Mink had a falling out and it really has him down on himself."

"A falling out about what?"

"Dave told Mink that everything they've been doing wasn't worth what happened to Staggs. Basically, he was telling him that he didn't want to live like that anymore."

"Yeah, well, if that's what Dave wants to do, Mink gotta respect that…"

"You're right, but that's not how Mink took it," she said, cutting him off. "Mink blew up on him after sniffing cocaine right in front of him."

"Mink sniffing cocaine? No," he said, shaking his head.

"Kamari, Dave wouldn't lie about nothing like that," she said defensively, while adjusting the baby who wouldn't keep still on her lap. "I would say something to Mink about it myself, but I went by his house the other day and he acted like I didn't exist."

"A'ight, I'ma talk to him and see what's up," he said, thinking about the way Mink had been acting lately as he rose up from the sofa.

"Kamari…" she started to say.

"What?" he said, staring at her.

"Nothing, never mind," she said, deciding against what she was going to say, which was for him to relay to Mink that she still loved him.

"Okay then, I'ma get back with you," he replied, heading for the door as she followed, baby in hand. "And if you need anything, don't hesitate to let me know."

"I won't. Thank you, Kamari."

"It's nothing," he replied with a smile before leaving.

CHAPTER 76

It was after midnight, and even at that late an hour, with the summer winding down, there were quite a few people out along Second Avenue. Parked in front of Ameina's building, Kamari sat behind the wheel of the Volkswagen Cabriolet with her seated in the passenger seat and his cousin Ski in the back, while Knox sat outside on the hood talking to some female on a cell phone.

"Why you ain't tell me that you knew Chew?" asked Ameina, staring over at him.

"What difference does it make?" he said, shrugging his shoulders.

"Did you know his cousin Rome?"

"No," he answered with a straight face.

"Who else you know that I know?"

"I don't know. Why don't you tell me everybody you know, and I'll let you know if I know any of them," he replied, making Ski laugh.

"You got a lot of shit with you," she said, shaking her head. "Anyway, when you going to take me to see about the coat?"

"What coat?"

"The coat you said you'd get me for Christmas."

"I ain't say no shit like that," he said, glancing over her head at the clear night sky.

"Kamari, yes, you did," she declared. "You said for me to put the money down on the one I wanted and you'd get it for me," she continued, talking about a six thousand dollar fur she wanted for the coming winter.

"When was this?" he questioned, looking at her with a puzzled expression.

"Why do we have to go through this every time I want something?"

"'Cause I don't remember, that's why."

"I'm talking about all the time, not just this time."

"Ain't no fucking all the time. Go 'head with the bullshit," he said, grinning over at her.

"Damn near," she responded, smiling. "With your tight ass."

"Oh, now I'm tight?" he said, as Ski laughed again.

"What are you laughing at?" Ameina asked, glancing back at Ski.

"I'm saying, y'all funny. All you do is argue," replied Ski, as he slouched across the back seat and smiled up at her.

"Yo, Knox, you ready?" called out Kamari.

"Where are you going?" she asked, turning to face him.

"To Brooklyn to drop Knox off," he answered, as Knox approached the passenger side door.

"I want to go," Ameina exclaimed.

"Nah, you ain't coming," he said, shaking his head.

"Why, if you only going to drop him off?"

"Cause I said so. Now come on so I can get outta here," he said, indicating with his hand for her to get out.

"Nope, that ain't good enough," she said, snatching the keys from the ignition.

"Yo, come on. I don't have time for the bullshit."

"Let me come then," she said, laughing at the expression on his face as he stared over at her.

"A'ight, you can come. Now give me the keys," he replied, holding out his hand.

"Nope, you said that too fast," she said, smiling.

"Give me the fucking keys, Ameina," he said, reaching out and grabbing her.

Opening the door and leaning out, she kept him from getting hold of her hand with the keys.

"Come on. I'm not playing with you," he said, getting angry as he tried to get the keys from her. "Fuck this shit," he cursed, as he started to get out the car and go around to her.

"Kamari, fuck it. Just let her come, 'cause we'll be here for...ever if y'all keep this up," stuttered Ski.

Knox, who had been standing outside the car waiting, climbed in back with Ski, knowing that Kamari wasn't going to remove her from the car or allow him to do it for him. When she finally gave him back the keys, they drove all the way to Brooklyn in silence, no music, no conversation. She had Kamari tight. This was the state of their relationship at the present, break up to make up, which would be the case when they arrived back at his place where the making up would begin.

CHAPTER 77

Mink was nowhere to be found. Kamari had gone to his house early in the morning figuring he would catch him before he woke, only to find out from his sister that he hadn't come home the night before. Now as he drove down 7th Avenue, he could see Tubah, Moose, and a few others shooting a game of dice on the corner. Pulling over, he waited on Tubah, who spotted him and made his way over to the car. Amongst the crowd shooting dice stood Myles, who stared over at them.

"Yo, I got some money for you," said Tubah, getting in the car with him.

"Yeah, we can do that later. Right now, I'm looking for Mink. Have you seen him?"

"Not since last night."

"Where?"

"At Wally's. Why? What's up?"

"Ain't nothing. I just need to see him on something. Yo, I'ma get with you later on that," he said, giving him five.

"Yeah, whatever, nigga. It's your call," replied Tubah, getting out of the car. He had seen Mink at Wally's snorting coke, but he wasn't going to speak on it if he didn't have to. Since Kamari didn't ask, he played it by the rules and minded his business.

CHAPTER 78

It was a long shot, Kamari thought, as he headed over to Wally's, which stayed open twenty-four hours, seven days a week, with females rotating on three eight-hour shifts. However, if what Dave said was true, than anything was possible. Coming to a stop in front of the club, he spotted Mink's black Milano parked a few cars down. Parking, he went inside the dimly lit club where two females performed onstage to a crowd of about four, while the bartender sat behind the bar reading a newspaper. Standing by the door, he scanned the place for Mink, picking out a figure with two females at the far end of the club. Despite the club being empty, if Kamari had not been searching for him, Mink would not have been detected in the shadowy corner in which he found him when he approached.

"Yo, Mink, what's up with you?" Kamari asked, while looking down at him as one of the topless females was bent over giving him head. The other sat on the opposite side of him snorting cocaine from a folded bill.

"Hay, look, ladies, it's my nigga Kamari," he said, smiling up at him as the female rose from his lap and wiped her mouth.

"What the fuck is you doing?" Kamari asked, as he fanned a hand at the whole scene of cocaine laid out on the table and the two cokehead whores all over him like leeches.

"All of this, this ain't nothing. You should have been here earlier," he answered, tweaking his nose as he laid back in the chair and placed his arms around the two females, who laughed in response.

"A'ight, let's go. We're outta here."

"We?" Mink said, glancing around. "Who you come with?" he asked, and as if on cue, the two females began laughing.

"Yo, I'm not joking with you, Mink. It's time to be out."

"I'm not going no fucking place. This is what I do. You go; we'll meet up later and do what you do," he said with a smirk, as the female who had been giving him head put her arms around him, as if to say he was not going anywhere.

"Yeah, we're leaving right now," Kamari replied, moving toward him. "Watch it," he said to the female holding onto him. "Get the fuck out the way, you cokehead bitch," he shouted, taking hold of her arm and slinging her from the chair out of his way.

"Hay, what the hell's going on over there?" yelled the bartender, drawing everyone's attention to them.

315

"Come on," said Kamari, ignoring the bartender and grabbing Mink by the arm.

"Get the fuck off me," shouted Mink, standing up, a .357 visible in the waist of his pants as he shoved him.

Gathering himself, Kamari rushed back at him. Mink dipped low and tried to scoop him up by the legs, but Kamari took hold of him by the neck and spread his legs while getting low to keep Mink from scooping him up.

"You ready to leave with me now?" Kamari said in between trying to catch his breath, as Mink grabbed him by the hip of his jeans and attempted to lift him again in the air. "Ah, ah," Kamari said, tightening his hold on him.

"Somebody break it up," yelled a female.

"Nobody better not touch me," shouted Kamari, looking around to see who was near him. "This is my fucking brother."

"We ain't no motherfucking brothers," yelled Mink.

"I love you like a brother, nigga."

"A'ight, Kamari, let me go. I ain't fucking playing with you."

"We're outta here together, right?"

"I'm telling you, Kamari," Mink warned.

"All you gotta…" he began, as Mink pulled the .357 from his waist and fired. "What the… fuck!" Kamari yelled, jumping back as the female screamed and Mink stood upright with the gun held at his side.

"Okay, that's it. I'm calling the cops," yelled the bartender.

"I told you to let me fucking go," said Mink, staring over at Kamari.

"Nigga, is you crazy" Kamari stated.

"If I was crazy, I would have shot you and not the floor."

"A'ight, do what the fuck you want. I'm out of here," shouted Kamari, making his way to the exit as the dancers and patrons looked on.

"That's what you should have done in the first place," yelled Mink after him, as one of the females he had been sitting with informed him that the bartender had called the police.

Snatching the bills of cocaine he had on the table, he headed for the exit. His burden was now heavier than when he had entered the night before.

317

CHAPTER 79

At Faison's Roundtable, the name Kamari jokingly gave the dining room table, he sat listening to Faison tell him how he took some girl out on an extravagant date.

"So I took her to Tavern on the Green in Central Park," narrated Faison.

"You stay tricking," replied Kamari, smiling over at him.

"Yo, bee, you know what they say, 'what's the use of getting it if you can't experience new things with it.'"

"Okay, how much did the experience cost you?"

"Two thousand," he answered, dipping his head in a mock gesture of shame.

"Two G's for what?"

"Food. It was alright, but the next day, I was sick as a dog."

"What about the girl? Did she get sick?"

"I don't know. I was too sick to call and find out," he said with a laugh.

"Bet you won't go there no more," Kamari replied, thinking that for two thousand dollars he should have been able to just roll over and ask her.

Then again, he wasn't sure if Faison could get it up since he was paralyzed. Having seen various females come by his apartment, he'd asked Ameina, who laughed and said she didn't know neither.

"Nah, bee, they won't get my money no more. Anyway, here's the money," he said, sliding a brown bag set inside a plastic grocery bag across the table. "It's $38,000. I still have one left. Travis is going to come get it tomorrow. So, see me tomorrow night."

"A'ight," answered Kamari, as the buzzer sounded.

"Get that for me."

Kamari got up and went over to the intercom system. "Who is it?" he asked, speaking into its speaker. "Somebody named Paul," he told Faison, repeating the name given.

"Buzz him up. That's my man, Paul Sands."

"Yeah, well, I'ma be out," he replied, hitting the buzzer.

"Yo, chill for a few. I want you to meet him. He sings."

319

"A'ight," Kamari said, cracking the door and returning to his seat.

"Come on over here, Paul, and blow something for my peoples," said Faison, smiling excitedly as he came through the door.

Paul, a neatly dressed and well-groomed dude in expensive shoes, walked over and stood beside Faison, smiling.

"I was telling my man, Kamari, about you. Let him hear something."

"How are you?" said the soft-spoken Paul, exchanging greetings with Kamari. "What do you want to hear?" he asked, facing Faison.

"You make anything sound good, so it don't matter," he replied eagerly.

With that, Paul began to sing, his voice deep and full, vibrating off the walls, filling the apartment. Kamari listened vaguely, though acknowledging that he could blow, which Faison raved about as he sung. Kamari sat politely listening as Faison tried to sell him on the idea of co-managing Paul, which required paying for studio time to prepare a demo and other expenses needed in the pursuit of acquiring a record deal. All this Kamari sat politely through, but his thoughts were on the incident that took place earlier between him and Mink.

"So what's up? You interested?" asked Faison.

"I'll think about it and let you know," he said, getting up and leaving.

Faison had come to understand that 'I'll think about it' from Kamari meant no.

CHAPTER 80

Cruising up 135th Street in his black Milano, Mink came to a halt behind a van at a red light on Amsterdam. Glancing around, he pulled a vial of cocaine from his pocket. Removing the cap, he sprinkled some on the back of his hand and snorted it. The light turned green, and the van proceeded on 135th as Mink made a right onto Amsterdam, heading uptown. For him, cruising this area had become like a ritual after the death of Staggs, and he treated it as such, always in deep concentration, tight jawed, a quiet rage simmering inside of him as he scanned the faces of people he passed.

Between 138th and 139th Streets on the downtown side, he spotted a familiar face, the sight of which made him grip the steering wheel as the rage inside of him boiled over. He literally had to restrain himself from slamming on the brakes and jumping out the car. He continued past the intersection of 139th while glancing back, not wanting to lose sight of the source of his furry. He came to a stop and waited for a break in traffic. When it came, he made a U-turn and double-parked on the corner of 139th. With the engine running, he stared intensely at the face of a man who stood on the sidewalk near the corner of 138th conversing with two other men.

"It's him," he said to himself, removing a .357 from between the side of the seat.

He then proceeded to exit the car as the man made his way toward a canary yellow Porsche, in which a woman sat in the passenger seat. Removing his hand from the door handle, he placed the gun in his lap, then put the car in drive and crept forward while rolling down the passenger window.

The man paid no attention to the black Milano rolling toward him alongside the parked cars as he walked around the back of the Porsche with his keys in hand. Mink watched, fingering the trigger of the .357 and tightening his grip on the handle, as he descended down on the man who was now coming out from behind the Porsche and into the street. No longer able to contain his rage, Mink stepped on the gas, causing the tires to spin before the car lurched forward, hitting the man as he spun around and tried to get out of the way. With a thump, the impact of the car broke both the man's legs, propelling him up onto the hood before he rolled onto the ground a few feet in front of his Porsche as the woman looked on in shock.

Coming to a screeching stop, Mink jumped out of the car and took a shot at the two approaching men who the man had been talking to, forcing them to scramble for cover as he trotted around the front of his car to where the man had fallen.

In the passenger seat, the woman crouched down in fear for her life, staring over the dashboard as Mink walked up to where the man lay crumbled on the ground. Looking down at the man who was still conscious and moaning in pain, Mink leveled the barrel of the .357 at his head.

"Remember me?" he said, as the terrified man stared wide-eyed up at him.

Mink pulled the trigger twice in succession. The bullets shattered his head on the ground causing blood to splatter on Mink. Ignoring the screams of the woman who had forgotten her fear in light of what she had just witnessed, Mink ran back to his car and pulled off, leaving behind an unidentifiable heap of carnage as he turned down 138th Street against traffic.

CHAPTER 81

"Hay Sal, you ever score with that blonde down at the courthouse you took out?" asked Officer Briggs, speaking to his partner who was doing the driving as they sat in traffic waiting on a light.

"I told you about it."

"When? I don't recall you telling me."

"At the bar last..." he began, as the crackle of a gunshot startled him."Sounds like it came from up ahead. Radio it in," he said, as the traffic started moving and two more shots rang out. "There's our man two blocks up," he added, switching on the sirens as they passed the 135th intersection on Amsterdam.

"I see him," said Briggs, watching Mink as he jumped in his car and took off. "This is car 22 in pursuant of a gunman, black male, driving a black Alfa Romero Milano, on Amsterdam and 138th heading towards Hamilton and Broadway. Send paramedics to the scene at 138th and Amsterdam; we have a possible victim," he yelled into the radio, while he watched a crowd form around someone laid out in the street as they turned down 138th after Mink.

325

CHAPTER 82

Mink heard the sirens as he turned down 138th, and though they weren't yet behind him, he couldn't take a chance with getting stuck at a light on Broadway. So, he decided he'd turn onto Hamilton against traffic and take 139th over to Riverside where he could get on the highway. Having been chased by the police hundreds of times in stolen cars and never getting caught, he felt confident that he would get away, and he probably would have had it not been for two elements working against him.

One was a cab double-parked near the corner of Hamilton and 138th, which turning onto Hamilton he easily avoided by swirving left where the second element came into play. Coming at him was a U-haul truck, and as he cleared the cab, he tried to whip back to the right as the truck skidded into him, sideswiping the rear end of the car. The back end of the car fishtailed, nipping the front end of the cab as Mink, in an effort to avoid crashing, whipped the steering wheel back to the left, causing the Milano to three-sixty into another on coming car as Briggs and his partner neared the intersection of 138th and Hamilton.

CHAPTER 83

"Ma, I'm staying at Kamari's tonight," said Ameina, as her and Kamari stood in the doorway of the living room where her mother sat watching television. "Ma, did you hear a word I said?" she asked, moving into the living room to get her mother's attention.

"I'm sorry, Mena," apologized her mother, not taking her eyes from the screen of her floor model television. "But these people are getting crazier by the day. I tell you, judgment day is coming, baby."

"Ma, what are you talking about?" asked Ameina, glancing at the screen.

"Some fool done killed a man over on Amsterdam in front of everybody."

"Yeah?" replied Ameina, taking a seat next to her mother on the sofa.

"Yep, ran him over and shot him to death. They talking about it right now," she said, pointing at the screen where a lady holding a microphone was talking.

Kamari who had remained in the hall came in to look, also.

327

Again, to update you on this late breaking story; about thirty minutes ago, at approximately 11:05 p.m., police say a man driving a 1988 black Alfa Milano...

Kamari's heart began to race at the mention of a black Milano. He had went looking for Mink after leaving Faison's to settle their differences, realizing that Mink had not tried to shoot him. Not to mention, he was high on cocaine at the time. Also, Kamari had acted on emotions instead of thinking the situation through. He treated Mink like he was a child, trying to force him to leave the club. He was wrong, and that's what he went to tell him. Now, as he stood listening to the woman on the television, he couldn't believe what he was hearing.

...hit a man on the corner of 138th and Amsterdam. Stopping, he exited his vehicle, firing on friends of the victim who witnessed him get hit and tried to come to his aid. Witnesses say the driver, who was described as a black male between the ages of nineteen and twenty-five, and wearing dark-colored clothing and a baseball cap, proceeded over to where the victim laid and fatally shot him several times. A nearby patrol car in the area witnessed the assailant fleeing the scene and gave chase down 138th onto Hamilton, where the assailant lost control of his vehicle, crashing into oncoming traffic before colliding into parked cars right here on Hamilton and 138th...

Kamari's hands began to sweat as he stood stiff as a board, bracing himself for the worst as the news anchor pointed and the camera zoomed in on what remained of Mink's car.

...Witnesses say the assailant then climbed out of the window of his wrecked vehicle and fled down 138th between Hamilton and Amsterdam, where police say he could be hiding in a number of buildings...

"Ameina, let me speak to you for a minute," Kamari said, not needing to hear anymore. It was Mink and he had to go and help him.

"Yeah, what's wrong?" she asked, following him into the hall.

"Yo, we're gonna have to do this another time. I gotta go," he said, turning to leave.

"Wait. What do you mean another time?" she started to complain, taking hold of his arm as he reached for the door.

When he turned to face her, the look on his face told her that now was not the time for one of her 'you don't give me no time' tantrums. She released his arm and he left, leaving her standing at the door. Glancing at the television, the newswoman was recapping the story of the shooting, and Ameina knew that whatever was happening over on

Amsterdam was the reason behind the look in Kamari's eyes that had given her a chill.

CHAPTER 84

Climbing through the window of the wreck, Mink spotted the patrol car bending the corner at 138th and come to a screeching stop, its path blocked by the truck and cab. Jumping to the ground, while clinging onto his .357, he ran down 139th, as Officer Briggs exited the patrol car and took to the sidewalk after him.

Mink dashed across the street towards one of the buildings, as another patrol car was bearing down on him from Broadway. It seemed to Mink as if the police were everywhere, the sound of their sirens closing in on him from all angles. Entering the building, he ran through the lobby to the end of the hall, opened the backdoor, and ran down a flight of stairs and out into the dimly lit alley. Pausing for a brief second, he took in his surroundings. There were residents on both 139th and 140th, and the only way out was through one of those buildings that lined both sides of the alley.

Mink resumed running down the alley, sirens blaring in the distance all around him. He ran up to the back door of another building on 139th Street thinking if he doubled back they wouldn't expect it. Entering the lobby, which was empty he sprinted to the front entrance and peered out. He saw police flooding into the block from both ends. Quickly he retreated back into the alley and entered the back door of one of the buildings on 140th again the lobby was empty so he raced to the front entrance and stepped out. There were two patrol cars working their way down 140th, one from Hamilton and the other from Amsterdam with searchlights scanning the buildings. Officers on foot with flashlights and guns drawn cautiously ran in and out of the buildings.

Knowing he had to make a move, Mink tucked the gun away in his waistband and sprinted out into the street for the building directly across from him. Spotting him, several officers shouted for him to stop as the patrol cars accelerated toward him. Reaching the building, he swung open the door, ran straight for the backdoor and out into the alley, where he ran as fast as he could down the alley and entered a building on the corner of 140th and Amsterdam. Coming through the backdoor into the lobby, he startled a woman entering her 1st floor apartment. Running over to her he drew his gun and grabbed hold of her as she tried to make it into her apartment.

"Shut up. I'm not going to hurt you," he commanded in a low voice, his face covered in sweat as he pushed her through the door, shutting it behind him.

"Linda, what's…" said a man, stopping cold in his tracks as he stepped into the hall and saw Mink standing beside the woman, who was his wife, with a gun pointed at her head.

"Shhh, don't say a word. Take three steps toward me and stop."

The man did as he was told.

"Good. Now nobody has to get hurt, and that's if everybody does like I say. No lying. Now, who else is in the apartment?" he asked, starring wide-eyed down the hall at the man, an affect caused by a combination of cocaine and his adrenaline.

"Our two children are sleeping in their rooms. Look, my man..."

"Hold up, don't 'my man' me. Just answer my questions, no more no less," he said, cutting him off. "The kids are sleeping. That's good. They don't even gotta know I was here. Now, are you sure there is nobody else here?"

"Yes, and that's the truth," answered the man, his concern for his family obvious by the look on his face.

CHAPTER 85

Driving down Madison, Kamari turned up 125th Street, the momentary delays in traffic due to the lights annoying him as he tried to make it to the area of the shooting. He didn't understand what would provoke Mink to murder someone in the view of so many witnesses the way he did. He just hoped he got away or he found him before the police. Weaving around a car that was moving too slowly for him, his cell phone began to ring, adding to the annoyance around him. He started not to answer it, and probably wouldn't have if he hadn't gotten stuck at a light on 8th Avenue. Snatching the phone up from the passenger seat, he answered it.

"Yeah," he said, his filled voice with frustration.

"Damn, nigga, you sound like you the one getting chased by the police."

"Yo, what the fuck is wrong with you? And where you at?" he shouted into the phone, smiling at Mink's ability to make light of the most difficult situations, and because hearing his voice meant he was safe.

"Yo, I got the motherfucker! I took care of it. I told you I would, nigga. I told you," he rambled on, as if each word bore the weight of his burdens, and through speaking, he was freeing himself of them.

334

"Mink, I can't understand you. What are you talking about?" he asked, continuing up 125th Street.

"The motherfucker from the spot…Kenny, Staggs, Cory… it was his fault. I got him! I told you I'd make it right. I told you."

"Yeah, my nigga, I hear you," Kamari replied, realizing what he was saying, and moved by Mink's commitment to their fallen friends and the memories it invoked of their tragic endings.

Although the man Mink murdered had played a part in the events that led to their deaths, it was Mink who had cast the first stone. Yet, by the laws of the streets, it was a form of closure in that he had finished what he started.

"Mink, look, this thing is all over the news. Where are you?" he asked, making a right onto Amsterdam.

"I guess it's true that everybody gets their fifteen minutes. This must be mine."

"Yo, Mink, stop playing. This shit is serious. Now, where the fuck are you?"

"I'm in an apartment building on the corner of 140th and Amsterdam."

"I ain't even gonna ask how you pulled that off."

"All you need to know is I ain't have to hurt nobody to do it," he replied, glancing over at his captors who were listening to his every word.

"A'ight, call back in five minutes. I'm on my way to you," he said, disconnecting the call.

CHAPTER 86

Standing in the living room, Mink placed the phone down and stared over at the couple whose home he had invaded. Walking the short distance over to the television, he turned it to the news.

"Damn, all that for me? You would think I killed the President," he said, backing away from the television so that he kept the couple in view.

The police had 139th and 140th sealed off from Hamilton to Amsterdam. They weren't allowing anyone in or out the blocks, and from what he could see on the screen, there had to be like two or three precincts swarming around in the blocks. Removing a vial of cocaine from his pocket, he made his way over to the window, snorting the cocaine as he went. Peeping through the window curtain, he could see the police barricade at the corner of 140th and Amsterdam with two police cars in front. It would only be a matter of time before they started going from door to door, he thought to himself. Turning around he finished off the rest of the cocaine. The couple stared up at him from the sofa, believing him to be a drugged- out lunatic. As if reading their minds, he smiled and headed for the phone.

CHAPTER 87

While turning off 138th back on to Amsterdam towards 139th where traffic moved at a snail's pace with curious motorist looking on at the spectacle, which was like something out of a movie, Kamari shook his head in amazement. Just then, his phone began to ring.

"Yo, it's crazy out here," he informed Mink, as he answered the phone.

"Tell me about it. Where you at now?"

"I'm coming up alongside the building you're in."

"I can see you," he said, moving back to the window and glancing out.

"Yo, maybe you should lay down on this one. The odds are against you major this time. We got money for good lawyers," reasoned Kamari turning down 140th.

"The odds have always been against me. It's the only way I know how to play the game. Now, tell me where to meet you at."

"A'ight, I'm heading down 140th towards St. Nicholas Terrace. There's a park one block over here that you can cut through to St. Nicholas Avenue. I can park on St. Nicholas Avenue and wait for you in the park, unless you can think of something else."

"One block to the park, that's it?"

"Yeah, that's it. One block, my nigga," Kamari said encouragingly, despite the doubts he had. "Just give me five minutes to be where I gotta be.

"Okay, that'll work, and Kamari?" said Mink, pausing as he stared over at the couple on the sofa.

"Yeah, I'm here."

"You think I'll be a good father?"

"What, nigga? Hell fucking yeah! The best."

"A'ight, I'm on my way," he said, hanging up.

CHAPTER 88

"There he goes!" shouted one of the officers from the 140th and Amsterdam barricade, as he pointed to a figure meeting the description of the suspect.

He jumped out of the 1st floor apartment window onto Amsterdam and ran out into the traffic laced street. The officer and his fellow officers took off after him, some on foot and some in patrol cars.

Mink watched from the window as the woman, who was tied up on the sofa, sat in fear while her husband ran toward 139th, staying in traffic like Mink had told him to avoid being shot at. When the last officer from the 140th barricade passed the window, Mink quickly dropped down from the window onto the sidewalk unnoticed and proceeded at a normal pace across the street, as officers from the 139th barricade cut the woman's husband off and forced him to the ground in the middle of the street.

Mink turned down 140th toward the park, as officers responding to the radio call, who had been on 140th between Hamilton and Amsterdam, came bursting from around the corner onto Amsterdam. Mink caught the eye of one of them, who stopped and stared suspiciously at him. Feeling someone's eyes on him, Mink made the mistake of glancing back, and found himself staring into the face of Officer Briggs.

"Hay, you," Officer Briggs yelled, drawing his gun as Mink broke out into a run.

Office Briggs chased after him, gun in one hand and radio in the other, as he yelled for back up.

CHAPTER 89

Kamari stood near a tree in St. Nicholas Park about twenty yards or so from the 8th Avenue entrance, looking in the direction of Amsterdam from which Mink would be coming. The park was empty, void of the students from nearby City College who occupied it during the day, early evening hours, and sometimes even into the wee hours of the night, but not on this night.

"Come on, Mink," he whispered to himself, glancing around as sirens sounded over on Amsterdam, a sign that Mink was on his way.

As if on cue, Mink came running down 140th, weaving through traffic as he crossed Convent onto St. Nicholas Terrace with Officer Briggs running several yards behind him. Nearing a bend in the road where St. Nicholas Park was located across from City College Mink pulled up into the gap of a fence that lined College concealing himself instead of continuing to the park.

Looking on in confusion, Kamari took two steps away from the tree and waved, thinking that maybe Mink didn't see him. In that same instance, Officer Briggs appeared from around the fence and what took place next played out in Kamari's head before it even happened.

Mink was not planning to meet him in the park, a realization that hit Kamari as hard as the .357 slug Mink fired into the officer's chest. By the time the second one hit him, sending him flailing back into the street, Kamari was numb to everything that followed.

Mink ran across the street and made a futile attempt for the chest-high fence that sectioned off the park, as patrol cars came to a screeching stop in front of the fallen officer, followed by officers on foot, all of whom opened fire on Mink more out of anger than duty. Mink's back arched forward as bullets riddled him from behind, sending him to his knees in a shower of his own blood, before he fell face forward into the fence and slid to the ground.

Later, when asked what he remembered most about the incident, Kamari wouldn't say the way Mink pulled up when he realized he couldn't get away and took out the man responsible for his failed escape. Nor would he mention that when countless rounds struck Mink from behind, he didn't cry out. No, it wouldn't be any of that, for he had known that side of Mink his whole life. Kamari would only speak on the last conversation he had with his friend before he was killed.

You think I'll be a good father?

What, nigga? Hell fucking yeah! The best.

Epilogue

CHAPTER 90

On October 19th of that year, Shonda gave birth to Mink's son two months after his death. He weighed eight pounds and ten ounces. Kamari was there and looking at Mink's son through the nursery window. He couldn't help but imagine Mink as a baby, born with the same innocence, and was sadden by the afterthought of the similarities between the birth of father and son. 'Cause like Mink, his son would also never know his father.

Shonda had handled Mink's death well, as if she had come to terms with it before it happened. At the funeral, she stood strong and proud, earning the respect and admiration of everybody there, including Sandy, who Mink had put second to her. Kamari had attended, having chosen the image of his friend resting in a coffin opposed to that of him being gunned down.

At the hospital, seeing Shonda holding her and Mink's son for the first time, Kamari knew her strength at the funeral had not been for her, but for the sake of her unborn child. Because holding him in her arms, she broke down and cried tears of sorrow and joy. Sorrow for the lost of the young man she loved and joy for his son, whom she had brought safely into the world knowing that through him, his father would live on. She named him Joseph Mink Stevens. Joseph, a name chosen by her and her mother from the Bible meaning "he who finds favor", gave them hope that her son would find favor in a world his father had not.

"Give me ten minutes," Kamari said to Knox who was driving a black Maxima as her pulled to a stop in front of Shonda's project building on 7th Avenue in Mount Vernon.

"Take your time," he replied as Kamari exited with a small Louis Voitton bag in hand.

Making his way to the building Kamari nodded at a few teenagers hanging out front before disappearing inside where he caught the elevator up to Shonda's tenth floor apartment. Knocking on the door he waited for someone to answer. "Shonda, look whose here. What's up Kamari," said Jackie smiling as she opened the door and held it ajar.

"Same old same 'O', you know," he answered stepping inside as she closed the door behind him.

"Hey Kamari, we haven't seen you in awhile," yelled Tammy from where she sat next to Shonda on the coach in the living room holding her son.

"Yeah, come on in here and sit down," exclaimed Shonda with a smile.

"Nah, I can't stay long I got somebody downstairs waiting on me," he said stepping just inside the room where to his right Brenda sat holding little Mink.

"What, you came to see your god-son," she shouted grinning up at him as she handed him the baby while the rest of them looked on smiling.

"What's up little man," he cood bending and taking him into his arms. Mink's son was beautiful and it pained Kamari that he never got to see the beauty he was capable of creating. His skin was a blend of Shonda's mocha and Mink's which made for a fiery brown. He had Mink's intense dark eyes, a head full of curly black hair, and unlike most babies with their fat baby faces, his was one defined in definition; character even Kamari thought as he held him. In all he was something special for many different reasons to those who loved Mink. "Here you go," he said handing him back to Brenda. "Shonda let me speak to you for a minute," he exclaimed stepping out into the hall as she rose to join him.

346

"Yeah, what is it," she asked as she stood before him.

"Here take this," he said handing her the Louis Voitton bag.

"What's that," she said not taking it, but rather staring at it as he held it out to her.

"Some money for you and the baby, and some numbers to get in touch with me if y'all ever need anything," he answered continuing to hold the bag out for to take.

"I can't take your money Kamari, we're all right."

"Come on Shonda, Christmas is right around the corner and your starting school in January," he reasoned.

"How you know all that," she asked narrowing her eyes at him with a smirk.

"I called before I came and spoke to your mother. Just take it please, I have to go."

"My mother has a big mouth," she exclaimed shaking her head. "How much is it, it looks kind of bulky."

"A couple of hundred in small bills," he answered gesturing for her to accept it.

"God, all right," she exhaled with a laugh at his unwillingness to accept no for an answer as she took the bag from him. "Thank you, but this is it Kamari, were going to be all right."

"Yeah I know. That's all I want," he replied opening the door behind him and backing out as her girlfriends hearing him leaving shouted their good-byes. "Later," he said winking at Shonda as he shut the door and headed for the stairs, not wanting to get stuck waiting on the elevator. Entering the staircase he heard Shonda calling after him. Ignoring her, he continued on down the stairs smiling. He knew Shonda was trying to put her life in perspective for the sake of her son. Disassociating her-self with the way she used to live, hanging out, partying, and the type of men she use to mess with like Mink. Though she was still attracted to the image of a man like Mink, and though loving him had been hard and painful, a pain that still ran deep. She would do it all again if it weren't for her son. Now she was a mother first and a woman second so for that purpose she had to suppress her attraction to men like the father of her son. She would make sure he knew about his father and all the things, bad and good, that made him the man he had been; the man she loved. But she would see to it that he learned from his father mistakes and become the man he never got a chance to be; and for this she would sacrifice.

CHAPTER 91

Outside the building Knox sat amused behind the wheel of the Maxima rocking his head to the sounds of Bob Marley's "Buffalo Soldiers" as he watched the teenage boys who had been in front the building move out into the street up ahead of him while playfully slap boxing with one another. In the background a black Chevey Blazer with light tented windows coasted up to the light on 4th Street near the park then quickly accelerated bending the corner up 7th Avenue against traffic toward the teenagers and Knox as a gray Crown Victorian sped out of the parking-lot of Shonda's building just ahead the Blazer and headed in the same direction, toward Knox. In confusion Knox quickly glanced around and spotted several more cars speeding down 7th Avenue on behind him from the 3rd Street end. The driver of the Crown Victorian rapidly beat its horn sending the startled teenagers scattering from the street as it roared down on Knox. Quickly Knox scurried from behind the wheel over to the passenger side door and leaped from the Maxima in an attempt to make it to the building to Kamari but was greeted by several agents storming down the walkway of the building toward him with guns and assault rifles pointed at him as they shouted and screamed.

"Freeze FBI!!! On the ground!!! Don't move!!! Hands on your head! FBI!!! On the ground!!! Down!!! Down!!! Down!!! FBI!!!" All at once. Knox just froze and threw his

349

hands up in the air as what seemed like a fleet of cars skidded to a stop all around him and a new round of screaming begin as they exited their cars. Then several agents unnecessarily threw Knox face down to the ground and placed their knees in his back while several more handcuffed him.

CHAPTER 92

Nearing the bottom of the stairs Kamari turned at a landing. "Pardon me," he said accidently bumping into someone coming up the stairs.

"Watch where---," begin Miles pausing in mid-sentences at the sight of Kamari who in recognizing him held his eyes and smiled flatly. When Miles said nothing further Kamari nodded, moved pass him down the stairs to the lobby door and pulled open the door. In that instant time as he knew it froze with sound of gun fire behind him echoing like thunder rumbling across the heavens through the stairwell. Then the realization that he was falling gripped him with something beyond fear. He wanted desperately to grab hold of something to break his fall feeling that if he fell he would never get back up, but there was nothing, only the sense of lose. Of loosing something he never thought to value. Another gunshot irrupted and the bullet struck him as he hit the floor and in that moment; even as a siring pain begin to rip through his body beginning in his back it was clear in his mind what he was losing. Images begin to play in his mind at something far faster than light, and he could see himself as a little boy falling and hearing his mother yelling for him to get up. I can't he mouthed as he lay alone dying at the bottom of the stairwell.

CHAPTER 93

Out front the building local police tried to disperse the crowd that was beginning to gather as Knox laid face down on the ground with his hands cuffed behind his back, an army of federal agents and local police standing over him. "Let's get this one in the car," shouted the Agent in charge.

Two agents hoisted Knox up from the ground by his arms and started to escort him to a car as the sound of gun fire was heard coming from the building. All the agents immediately drew their guns and went on alert some dropping to the ground unsure if they were being shot at. "It's coming from inside the building," shouted a Housing Cop.

At that moment Miles emerged from the building unaware of the happenings outside as if he hadn't heard the gunshots something the agents immediately took notice of. The instant Knox saw Miles the day he knocked him out for a thousand dollars wagered by Kamari came back to him. Miles looked up. "You, don't move," shouted one of the agents as every law enforcement officer present drew their gun. A split second of indecision overcame Miles as he stood like a deer trapped in the glare of headlights; only for him it was the barrel of nearly thirty guns. Then he broke into a run toward the rear of the building. He may have gotten away or at least lead the police on a good chase but he made the mistake of reaching for the gun in an effort to toss it and they opened fire on him. Bullets struck him from all angles halting him in stride as his body twisted into a contorted dance, the gun falling from his hand before he fell dead along the side of the building.

"In the building, I need all available men inside the building. We have a possible victim," shouted the commanding agent as him and several others rushed into the building.

The End

I want to take this moment to thank you the reader for your support and ask that you write a review online at Amazon, Barnes & Nobles, Goodreads etc, wether positive or negative it's all welcome. Also be sure to check out my work as a Director on Reelhouse.com; where my short film "The Death of a Prince" can be rented and streamed on mobile devices, apple tv or any internet compatable TV. In closing feel free to follow me @ar_hilton on Instagram, @ARHilton on Twitter, A.R.Hilton on Facebook, A.R.Hilton on Goodreads and I can be contacted at a.r.hilton01@gmail.com. I look forward to engaging you the reader in conversation.

Sincerely,

A.R.Hilton

www.ingramcontent.com/pod-product-compliance
Lightning Source LLC
Chambersburg PA
CBHW071220290326
41931CB00037B/1499